高校专门用途英语（ESP）系列教材

READING AND TRANSLATING IN EST TEXT
科技语篇阅读与翻译

主编　王均松
　　　陈　洁
编者　崔维霞

清華大學出版社
北　京

内 容 简 介

本教材共八个单元，内容涵盖宇宙探秘、航空航天、物理科学、材料科学、生物医学、自动化工程、人工智能、能源生态等领域。本教材的一个突出特色是读译结合，每个单元包括阅读和翻译两个板块，围绕同一主题设计任务并讲解相关技巧策略。两个板块彼此联系、相互补充，旨在帮助学生快速提升科技英语阅读和翻译能力。此外，所选语篇均来自国内外权威杂志和网站，语言地道、素材真实，具有时代性和趣味性，能够激发学习者的学习热情。本教材另配有参考答案和PPT课件，读者可登录"清华社英语在线"（www.tsinghuaelt.com）进行下载。

本教材适用于高校英语专业和非英语专业学生的选修课教学，也可作为研究生、科技工作者以及科技英语爱好者的学习和参考资料。

版权所有，侵权必究。举报：010-62782989，beiqinquan@tup.tsinghua.edu.cn。

图书在版编目（CIP）数据

科技语篇阅读与翻译 / 王均松，陈洁主编；崔维霞编者 . 一北京：清华大学出版社，2023.4
高校专门用途英语（ESP）系列教材
ISBN 978-7-302-62535-3

Ⅰ.①科… Ⅱ.①王… ②陈… ③崔… Ⅲ.①科学技术—英语—阅读教学—高等学校—教材②科学技术—英语—翻译—高等学校—教材 Ⅳ.① G301

中国国家版本馆 CIP 数据核字（2023）第 017661 号

责任编辑：方燕贝
封面设计：子 一
责任校对：王凤芝
责任印制：曹婉颖

出版发行：清华大学出版社
　　　　　网　　址：http://www.tup.com.cn, http://www.wqbook.com
　　　　　地　　址：北京清华大学学研大厦 A 座　　**邮　编**：100084
　　　　　社 总 机：010-83470000　　**邮　购**：010-62786544
　　　　　投稿与读者服务：010-62776969, c-service@tup.tsinghua.edu.cn
　　　　　质量反馈：010-62772015, zhiliang@tup.tsinghua.edu.cn
印 装 者：三河市人民印务有限公司
经　　销：全国新华书店
开　　本：185mm×260mm　　**印　张**：12.5　　**字　数**：233 千字
版　　次：2023 年 5 月第 1 版　　　　　　　**印　次**：2023 年 5 月第 1 次印刷
定　　价：58.00 元

产品编号：097593-01

前　言

进入 21 世纪，随着科技发展的日新月异，国际交流与日俱增，无论是阅读科技文献、发表科技论文，还是进行国际学术交流，都离不开英语这一重要的交流工具，科技英语的重要性日益突出。在传统的科技英语教学中，阅读和写作的重要性已得到广泛认可，而翻译却没有得到应有的重视。实际上，在科技文化交流中，翻译与阅读、写作具有同等重要的作用，很多科技知识的引进与传播都依赖于翻译。因此，提升学生的科技语篇阅读与翻译能力是外语教学中重要的任务之一。

在外语学习中，阅读与翻译的关系十分紧密。良好的阅读能力是进行翻译的前提和基础，如果阅读能力较差，语篇理解会容易出现偏差，那么就难以产出高质量的译文。反过来，翻译对阅读也具有推动和促进作用。为了达到良好的翻译效果，学习者必须对原文进行反复研读和深入理解，这无疑有助于阅读能力的提升。《科技语篇阅读与翻译》旨在满足英语学习者的实际需求，帮助他们通过阅读与翻译训练系统地掌握科技英语知识，提高运用科技英语的能力。

本教材具有以下四大特色：

1. 价值引领

本教材在"立德树人"的指导思想下，充分发挥外语课程的价值引领和育人功能，将价值塑造、知识传授和能力培养三者融为一体，在传授科技英语知识、培养阅读和翻译能力的同时，帮助学习者树立正确的世界观、人生观和价值观。在筛选语篇的过程中，本教材不仅采用了介绍国外先进科技成果的文章，同时选取了一些关于中国科技进步和伟大成就方面的文章，比如国人引以为豪的"中国天宫空间站"、获得诺贝尔医学奖的中国女科学家屠呦呦等。对这些语篇的学习以及讨论将有助于英语学习者建立"科技自信"和"文化自信"。

2. 题材广泛

本教材语篇均精心选自权威的科技期刊网站、专栏与科普读物，专业性强、知识面广。全书根据主题分为八个单元，涵盖宇宙探秘、航空航天、物理科学、材料科学、生物医学、自动化工程、人工智能、能源生态等领域。教材内容丰富，选材兼具时代性和趣味性，既突出当今时代科技进步为人类所做的贡献，同时贴近现实生活，激发学习者的英语学习热情。

3. 读译结合

读译结合是本教材的一个显著特点。阅读理解是翻译的基础和前提，翻译又可以促进对原文的理解，二者紧密相连、相辅相成。基于上述考虑，本教材的每个单元由阅读和翻译两个板块组成。阅读板块中的 Text 1 是一篇泛读文章，目的是训练学习者的信息检索能力；Text 2 是一篇精读文章，着重于培养学习者的推理判断、归纳分析、评价鉴赏等认知能力。翻译板块中的 Text 3 是一篇服务于译文修改任务的文章，旨在提高学习者的译文诊断和修改能力。此外，每个单元还设计了 Reading Tips 和 Translation Tips 部分，二者内容彼此联系、互为补充，有助于学习者更好地掌握并运用阅读和翻译技能。

4. 以评促译

"以评促译"是本教材提出的一个重要教学理念，即通过评价和修改译文来促进学习者的翻译学习。编者在长期的翻译教学过程中发现，学生互评修改可以激发他们学习的积极性和主动性，有利于培养其批判性思维，提升英语翻译能力。鉴于此，本教材在翻译板块设置了一项译文修改任务，即将存在问题的译文作为教学案例用于评价与修改，并提供了详细的评价反馈和修改意见，供学习者借鉴与参考。

本教材不仅适合高等院校的非英语专业本科生使用，还可以作为英语专业科技英语类课程的选修教材，甚至可以作为高校研究生、科技工作者以及英语爱好者学习和参考的材料。

限于编者水平有限，编写工作中难免存在疏漏与不足，热忱欢迎各位专家和读者批评指正。

编者
2023 年 2 月

Contents

CHAPTER 1   Mysterious Universe 1

Text 1 What Is Astronomy? 2
Text 2 The Solar System 7
Reading Tips 科技语篇的阅读策略 12
Text 3 The Big Bang: It Sure Was Big! 14
Translation Tips 科技语篇的翻译标准 23

CHAPTER 2   Aerospace Engineering 25

Text 1 James Webb Space Telescope 26
Text 2 China's Tiangong Space Station 31
Reading Tips 科技英语的词汇特点 36
Text 3 Ramjet Engine 39
Translation Tips 词义的选择与引申 47

CHAPTER 3   Physical Science 49

Text 1 How Maglev Trains Work 50
Text 2 The General Theory of Relativity 55
Reading Tips 科技英语中的数字用法 61
Text 3 The Echo-location in Bats 63
Translation Tips 科技英语倍数的翻译方法 70

CHAPTER 4   Materials Science 73

Text 1 Nanotechnology 74
Text 2 Graphene: The Magic Material 79

Reading Tips 科技英语的句法特点（一） ········· 84
Text 3 Small Lights with Big Potential ········· 87
Translation Tips 否定句的翻译方法 ········· 94

CHAPTER 5   Biomedical Science ········· 97

Text 1 Artemisinin: Discovery from the Chinese Herbal Garden ······ 98
Text 2 What Are Heat Shock Proteins? ········· 103
Reading Tips 科技英语的句法特点（二） ········· 108
Text 3 That Others May Live ········· 110
Translation Tips 状语从句的翻译方法 ········· 116

CHAPTER 6   Automatic Engineering ········· 119

Text 1 Drone Technology ········· 120
Text 2 3D Printing: What You Need to Know ········· 125
Reading Tips 事实与观点的区别 ········· 130
Text 3 Robots in Home and Telerobots ········· 132
Translation Tips 定语从句的翻译方法 ········· 139

CHAPTER 7   Artificial Intelligence ········· 141

Text 1 The Future of Information Technology and Artificial Intelligence ········· 142
Text 2 Augmented Reality and Virtual Reality ········· 147
Reading Tips 首/尾焦点与尾重原则 ········· 153
Text 3 Radio Frequency Identification ········· 155
Translation Tips 长难句的翻译方法 ········· 162

CHAPTER 8　Energy and Ecology ·············· 165

Text 1 Why Are Alternative Energy Sources the Future? ············ 166
Text 2 Moving to a Competitive Low-carbon Economy ············· 170
Reading Tips 科技语篇的主述位推进模式 ······························· 176
Text 3 Of Warming and Warning ·· 178
Translation Tips 科技语篇翻译的衔接与连贯 ·························· 185

Bibliography ·· 189

CHAPTER 1
Mysterious Universe

Introduction

The vast and mysterious universe looks quiet and lonely ostensibly, but there are numerous mazes and wonders hidden inside, which have aroused endless reveries and imaginations. The three texts in this chapter center on the theme of the mysterious universe. To be specific, Text 1 is a passage for fast reading, dealing with the discipline of astronomy; Text 2 is a passage for intensive reading, introducing the solar system and its eight planets; and Text 3 is a passage for translation, discussing the origin of the universe. The learning objective of this chapter is to familiarize the learners with the reading strategies for EST (English for Science and Technology) and the criteria for EST translation.

Lead-in Questions

1. "The universe is the vast empty space surrounding the planets and stars. It consists of dark matter, dark energy, stars, and galaxies." Does this statement match up to your idea about the universe?

2. What is your comment on the German philosopher Immanuel Kant's quote: "Two things fill the mind with ever new and increasing admiration and reverence, the more often and more steadily one reflects on them: the starry heavens above me and the moral law within me"?

Section A Fast and Intensive Reading

Text 1 What Is Astronomy?

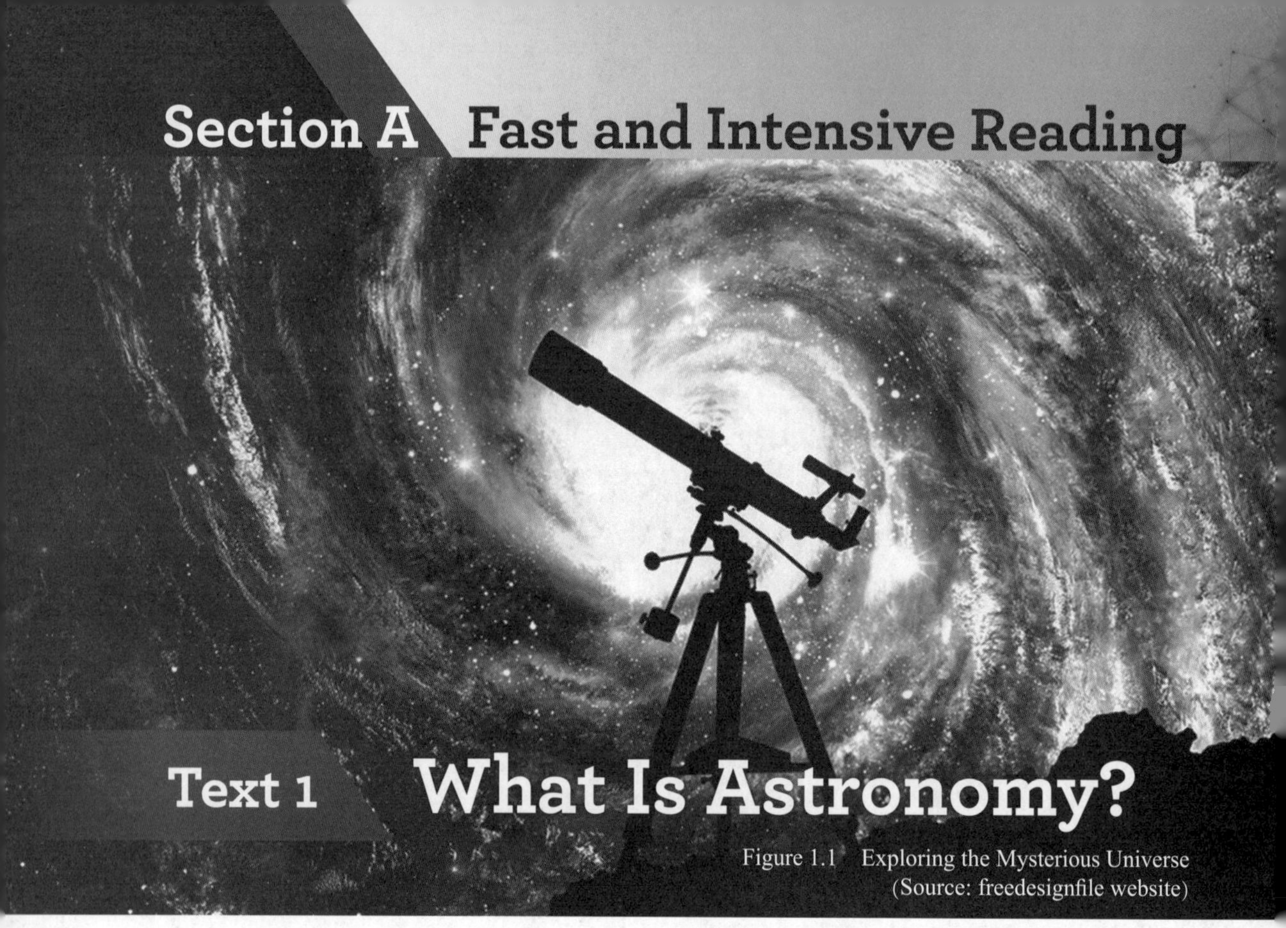

Figure 1.1 Exploring the Mysterious Universe
(Source: freedesignfile website)

A Astronomy is the study of the Sun, Moon, stars, planets, and other objects and phenomena in space. It has a long, rich history.

B Every night, using the science of astronomy, the entire universe can be revealed above us. Although at some point we've all had that "blanket of stars" moment, it is an illusion. The visible planets and the bright stars you can see with your eyes are mostly very close to us—in cosmic terms—but the night sky has incredible, almost unfathomable depth. Not only can our own galaxy, the Milky Way, be navigated and known but other galaxies can be probed using telescopes, on Earth and in space, and in various wavelengths of light from all kinds of cosmic objects. Here's everything you need to know about what astronomy is, what it's not, and how recent developments within the field of astronomy are making it more exciting than ever before.

C What does astronomy mean? A dictionary will tell you that it's the branch of science that deals with celestial objects, space, and the physical universe as a whole. Astronomy is the study of everything in the universe that's beyond our own planet's atmosphere. The planets in our own solar system, our own star the Sun, and the bright stars can all be seen with the naked eye. However, astronomy can go much deeper, taking advantage of telescopes and other

CHAPTER 1 Mysterious Universe

scientific instruments to study other stars and their planets in our galaxy, as well as distant galaxies beyond our own. It can gather clues about the nature of the physical, chemical, and biological universe itself.

D   Astronomers aren't stargazers. Or, at least, there's no longer any need for them to be. If you think an astronomer treks up mountains to spend night after night behind the eyepiece of a giant telescope, think again. These days telescopes can be controlled remotely, so it's common for modern astronomers to simply make requests for observations and then download computer-generated data and images the next morning for their analysis. That includes space telescopes like the Hubble Space Telescope.

E   People very often confuse astronomy with astrology. Every professional astronomer has had to hear someone say to them, "So you're an astrologer, right?" Astrology and astronomy are not the same thing, but they used to be. Observational astronomy can be traced back to Ancient Egypt and Mesopotamia as far back as 3,000 B.C., but the calculating of solar eclipses, the movements of the planets, and theories about how the night sky works were the jobs of ancient astrologers who presumed that celestial events and alignments had a direct impact on human affairs. Modern astrologers attempt to do something similar, making predictions about human lives based on pseudoscience. Astrology is not a science.

F   In the past century or so, astronomy has been broadly split into two camps—observational astronomy (using telescopes and cameras to collect data about the night sky) and theoretical astronomy (using that data to analyze, model, and theorize about how objects and phenomena work).

G   They complement each other, yet within these two broad categories modern astronomy includes many subsets, from astrometry to exoplanetology, that intrinsically overlap yet help explain the many things astronomers do. Here's what they all mean:

- **Astrometry:** This ancient branch of astronomy concerns precise calculations of the motions of the Sun, the Moon, and the planets. It includes predictions of solar and lunar eclipses, and meteor showers. It also includes exoplanetology, a relatively new and very exciting field that concerns itself with the discovery and characterization of planets outside of the solar system.

- **Planetary astronomy:** How did the solar system come to be? This is the central question penetrating planetary astronomy, which focuses on the formation, evolution, and death of planets, moons, and other objects. In the solar system, it also includes planetary geology.
- **Astrophysics:** Astrophysicists apply the laws and theories of physics to astronomical observations. It's an attempt to understand the mechanism behind how the universe was created and how it has and will evolve.
- **Astrochemistry:** Astrochemists study the composition and reactions of atoms, molecules, and ions in space.
- **Astrobiology:** This emerging and, for now, largely theoretical field of astronomy is the study of life beyond Earth.
- **Stellar astronomy:** The study of the life cycle and structure of the Sun and the stars, stellar astronomy concerns the classification and populations of stars.
- **Solar astronomy:** Galactic astronomers study our galaxy, the Milky Way, while extragalactic astronomers peer outside of it to determine how these groups of stars form, change, and die.
- **Cosmology:** Although it's sometimes used to mean astronomy, strictly speaking, cosmology refers to the science of the origin and nature of the universe. The key concept in cosmology is the Big Bang theory, the most widely accepted explanation of how the universe began. Cosmology also includes purely theoretical subjects including string theory, dark matter and dark energy, and the notion of multiple universes.

H All astronomy is the study of different wavelengths of the electromagnetic spectrum, which comprises radio, microwave, infrared, visible, ultraviolet, X-ray, and gamma rays. To get the full picture of what's out there, astronomers need to study various wavelengths of light.

I Optical astronomy is the study of celestial objects using telescopes and in visible light; all of the biggest telescopes on Earth are optical. Infrared light can be detected outside of the Earth's atmosphere by space-based observatories like the Hubble Space Telescope and the James Webb Space Telescope. Radio astronomy is the study of the sky in radio frequencies; radio telescopes detect and amplify radio waves from space.

CHAPTER **1** Mysterious Universe

J   However they observe the universe, astronomers only ever get a snapshot of the planets, stars, and galaxies they study. So, although there are dozens of different branches of astronomy, in practice many of them must overlap for an astronomer to get as full a picture as possible of objects that exist for millions to billions of years.

K   We're on the cusp of some tremendously exciting new technology that looks set to revolutionize astronomy. The most obvious is the James Webb Space Telescope, which from 2022 will probe the cosmos to uncover the history of the universe. Just as exciting are the Vera Rubin Observatory all-sky survey and the new generation of massive ground-based telescopes like the Extremely Large Telescope, which should all see "first light" in the mid-2020s. The Square Kilometer Array, the world's largest radio telescope, should also be operating by the late 2020s. Astronomers are about to see deeper into space to observe regions and objects never seen before.

(Source: Space website)

Notes

astrology: the study of the positions of the stars and the movements of the planets in the belief that they influence human affairs   占星术；占星学

Hubble Space Telescope: a space telescope that was launched into low Earth orbit in 1990 and remains in operation   哈勃太空望远镜

James Webb Space Telescope: The James Webb Space Telescope (JWST), previously known as Next Generation Space Telescope (NGST), is a flagship-class space observatory under construction and scheduled to launch in October 2018.   詹姆斯·韦伯空间望远镜

Mesopotamia: the region of Asia between the Tigris and Euphrates rivers   美索不达米亚［古希腊对两河（幼发拉底河和底格里斯河）流域的称谓，意为"（两条）河流之间的地方"］

Vera Rubin Observatory: Vera Rubin Observatory in Chile features an 8.4-meter telescope, a 3,200 megapixel camera, an automated data processing system, and an online public engagement platform.   薇拉·鲁宾天文台（位于智利，安装了世界上最大的天文数码照相机）

Exercises

Task A Identify the paragraph from which each of the following statements is derived. You may choose a paragraph more than once. Each paragraph in the above text is marked with a letter.

1. Generally speaking, there are two types of astronomy.
2. With the help of the latest telescopes, astronomers are expecting to probe deeper into the universe.
3. Even though astronomers have been studying the universe for a long time, they know just a little about it.
4. The study of the origin and nature of the universe is the focus of cosmology.
5. Astronomy can deal with the nature of the physical universe.
6. Many people wrongly take astronomers as astrologers.
7. The "blanket of stars" we often see with our eyes is an optical illusion.
8. The largest telescopes are optical so that they can detect light in outer space.
9. Astronomers can know the universe better by studying different wavelengths of lights.
10. Telescope data can be generated by its computer and sent to astronomers from afar.

Task B Work in groups to discuss the following topic and share your opinions with the class.

What Motivates Humans to Explore the Universe?

Have you ever wondered why humans devote considerable resources to studying celestial bodies beyond the Earth's atmosphere? Some may argue that it allows us to gain insights into the universe, uncover its origins, advance technological development, and spark a sense of awe and inquisitiveness. What are your own reasons for your stance on this matter?

Text 2 The Solar System

Figure 1.2 Planets in the Solar System
(Source: Pixabay website)

Solar system consisting of the Sun—an average star in the **Milky Way Galaxy**—and those bodies orbiting around it: 8 (formerly 9) planets with about 210 known planetary satellites; countless **asteroids**, some with their own satellites; comets and other icy bodies; and vast reaches of highly tenuous gas and dust known as the **interplanetary medium**.

The Sun, Moon, and brightest planets were visible to the naked eyes of ancient astronomers, and their observations and calculations of the movements of these bodies gave rise to the science of astronomy. Today the amount of information on the motions, properties, and compositions of the planets and smaller bodies has grown to immense proportions, and the range of observational instruments has extended far beyond the solar system to other galaxies and the edge of the known universe. Yet the solar system and its immediate outer boundary still represent the limit of our physical reach, and they remain the core of our theoretical understanding of the **cosmos** as well. Earth-launched space probes and landers have gathered data on planets, moons, asteroids, and other bodies, and this data has been added to the measurements collected with telescopes and other instruments from below and above Earth's atmosphere and to the

Milky Way Galaxy 银河系

asteroid 小行星

interplanetary medium 星际介质

cosmos 宇宙

information extracted from meteorites and from Moon rocks returned by astronauts. All this information is scrutinized in attempts to understand in detail the origin and evolution of the solar system—a goal towards which astronomers continue to make great strides.

Located at the center of the solar system and influencing the motion of all the other bodies through its gravitational force is the Sun, which in itself contains more than 99% of the mass of the system. The planets, in order of their distance outward from the Sun, are **Mercury**, **Venus**, Earth, **Mars**, **Jupiter**, **Saturn**, **Uranus**, and **Neptune**. Four planets—Jupiter through Neptune—have ring systems, and all but Mercury and Venus have one or more moons. **Pluto** had been officially listed among the planets since it was discovered in 1930 orbiting beyond Neptune, but in 1992 an icy object was discovered still farther from the Sun than Pluto. Many other such discoveries followed, including an object named **Eris** that appears to be at least as large as Pluto. It became apparent that Pluto was simply one of the larger members of this new group of objects, collectively known as the **Kuiper belt**. Accordingly, in August 2006 the International Astronomical Union (IAU), the organization charged by the scientific community with classifying astronomical objects, voted to revoke Pluto's planetary status and place it under a new classification called **dwarf planet**.

Any natural solar system object other than the Sun, a planet, a dwarf planet, or a moon is called a small body; these include asteroids, meteoroids, and comets. Most of the several hundred thousand asteroids, or minor planets, orbit between Mars and Jupiter in a nearly flat ring called the **asteroid belt**. The myriad fragments of asteroids and other small pieces of solid matter (smaller than a few tens of meters across) that populate interplanetary space are often termed meteoroids to distinguish them from the larger steroidal bodies. The solar system's several billion

Mercury 水星
Venus 金星
Mars 火星
Jupiter 木星
Saturn 土星
Uranus 天王星
Neptune 海王星
Pluto 冥王星

Eris 阋神星

Kuiper belt 柯伊伯带

dwarf planet 矮行星

asteroid belt 小行星带

CHAPTER 1 Mysterious Universe

comets are found mainly in two distinct reservoirs. The more-distant one, called the **Oort cloud**, is a spherical shell surrounding the solar system at a distance of approximately 50,000 astronomical units (AU)—more than 1,000 times the distance of Pluto's orbit. The other reservoir, the Kuiper belt, is a thick disk-shaped zone whose main concentration extends 30–50 AU from the Sun, beyond the orbit of Neptune but including a portion of the orbit of Pluto. (One astronomical unit is the average distance from Earth to the Sun—about 150 million km [93 million miles].) Just as asteroids can be regarded as rocky debris left over from the formation of the inner planets, Pluto, its moon Charon, Eris, and the myriad other Kuiper belt objects can be seen as surviving representatives of the icy bodies that accreted to form the cores of Neptune and Uranus. As such, Pluto and Charon may also be considered to be very large comet nuclei. The Centaur objects, a population of comet nuclei having diameters as large as 200 km (125 miles), orbit the Sun between Jupiter and Neptune, probably having been gravitationally perturbed inward from the Kuiper belt. The interplanetary medium—an exceedingly tenuous plasma (ionized gas) laced with concentrations of dust particles—extends outward from the Sun to about 123 AU.

Oort cloud 奥尔特云

As the amount of data on the planets, moons, comets, and asteroids has grown, so too have the problems faced by astronomers in forming theories of the origin of the solar system. In the ancient world, theories of the origin of Earth and the objects seen in the sky were certainly much less constrained by fact. Indeed, a scientific approach to the origin of the solar system became possible only after the publication of Isaac Newton's **laws of motion and gravitation** in 1687. Even after this breakthrough, many years elapsed while scientists struggled with applications of Newton's laws to explain the apparent motions of planets, moons, comets, and asteroids. In 1734, Swedish philosopher Emanuel Swedenborg

laws of motion and gravitation 运动和引力定律

proposed a model for the solar system's origin in which a shell of material around the Sun broke into small pieces that formed the planets. This idea of the solar system forming out of an **original nebula** was extended by the German philosopher Immanuel Kant in 1755.

original nebula
原始星云

(Source: Britannica website)

Exercises

Task A Decide whether the following statements are true (T) or false (F).

1. The solar system is composed of the Sun, nine planets, countless asteroids, comets and other icy bodies, and interplanetary medium.

2. The Sun, Moon, and brightest planets were invisible to the naked eyes of ancient astronomers.

3. The Sun locates at the center of the solar system and contains more than 99% of the mass of the solar system.

4. Four planets—Jupiter through Neptune—have ring systems and one or more moons.

5. Several billion comets are found mainly in two distinct reservoirs, namely the Oort shell and Kuiper belt.

Task B Choose the word or phrase which is closest in meaning to the underlined part in each sentence.

1. The Sun, Moon, and brightest planets were visible to the naked eyes of ancient astronomers, and their observations and calculations of the movements of these bodies <u>gave rise to</u> the science of astronomy.

   A. produced   B. attracted   C. operated   D. deduced

2. All this information is <u>scrutinized</u> in attempts to understand in detail the origin and evolution of the solar system—a goal towards which astronomers continue to make great strides.

   A. analyzed   B. scanned   C. searched   D. examined

3. It became <u>apparent</u> that Pluto was simply one of the larger members of this new group of objects, collectively known as the Kuiper belt.

   A. appealing   B. obscure   C. obvious   D. understandable

4. The Centaur objects, a population of comet nuclei having diameters as large as 200 km (125 miles), orbit the Sun between Jupiter and Neptune, probably having been gravitationally perturbed inward from the Kuiper belt.
   A. the number of   B. a number of   C. a group of   D. a portion of

5. In the ancient world, theories of the origin of Earth and the objects seen in the sky were certainly much less constrained by fact.
   A. enforced by   B. subject to   C. restricted by   D. provoked by

Task C Answer the following questions based on the text.

1. What is the solar system composed of?
2. Can you name the eight planets in order of their distance outward from the Sun?
3. Why is Pluto removed from the list of planets in the solar system?
4. What is the difference between asteroids and meteoroids?
5. What makes it possible for us to take a scientific approach to the origin of the solar system?

Reading Tips 科技语篇的阅读策略

科技语篇阅读是一项具有挑战性的任务，读者既要有通观全局的语篇意识，又要有准确理解具体信息的能力。掌握一定的阅读策略是加快阅读速度、提高阅读质量的重要手段。根据阅读目的的不同，科技语篇阅读可以分为浏览式阅读（skimming）、扫描式阅读（scanning）和精细式阅读（close reading）三种，下文将就其具体策略展开阐述。

1. 浏览式阅读

浏览式阅读是一种选择性阅读策略，目的是了解文章大意、主题思想、主要观点、研究发现等。换言之，浏览式阅读的主要目标是抓住文章的主旨大意。其具体策略技巧包括：

- **快速预览语篇**：首先快速浏览文章的标题、副标题、首尾段、表格和图表，或学术论文的摘要、关键词和结论，初步判断文章的主题是否与预想的一致、是否包含想要查找或了解的内容，从而从宏观上把握文本的主要内容和整体结构。
- **抓段落主题句**：主题句（topic sentence），也称为中心句，是对段落中心思想或主要内容的高度概括。它可以阐述作者的观点、看法或态度，并为该段落的展开提供依据。主题句通常位于段首或段尾，段落内其他句子则围绕主题句展开。重点阅读每个段落的主题句和主题词，可以帮助读者快速抓住段落大意及篇章脉络。

2. 扫描式阅读

扫描式阅读是为了寻找特定的信息而大致快速地扫读，主要用于解决或回答细节理解类问题，如寻找日期、地名、人名、数据等。扫描式阅读没有必要从头到尾、逐字逐句地阅读，而是通过找准定位词，快速地在文章内"寻找"出定位词，并结合上下文进行推理和判断，那么问题就会迎刃而解。其具体策略技巧包括：

- **利用章节标题**：在回答细节类问题时，因为已经有明确的目标对象，所以没有必要从头到尾通读文章。读者可以先利用章节标题等信息大致判断可能包含目标信息的段落或章节，再直接进入该部分进行扫读和查找，这样可以提高阅读效率。
- **利用提示词**：在扫读过程中，读者要留心与所寻找信息相关的提示词。这些提示词可能是题目中的关键词，如人名、地名、年代、数字等，也可能是与关键词密切相关的词汇或短语，如同义词等。例如，题目要求在文章中查找

the sales of Airbus'A-series in 2019，那么"2019"和Airbus'A-series就是提示词，读者可以根据这些提示词快速定位信息所在位置。

- **借助语境信息**：科技语篇中专业词汇占比较高，因此读者需要掌握借助语境信息猜测词义的能力。通常情况下，专业技术词汇首次出现时会在上下文中提供定义，或通过示例、比喻、对比等方式对其进行解释。有时，该词还会在上下文中被反复提及或以近义词的形式重述。因此，借助上下文语境进行分析和比较可以更加准确地判断出词义。另外，标点符号、逻辑关系词、语篇标记词等都有助于判断词义。

3. 精细式阅读

精细式阅读是指从词汇、句法、篇章逻辑结构等方面对阅读材料进行全面、深入的分析，将文章读懂、读透。细致、深入地阅读可以从根本上提升读者的语言水平和阅读理解能力。其具体策略技巧包括：

- **批注标记**：批注标记指通过添加下划线、突出显示或做注释的方式阅读文本。这种方法可以帮助读者加深对材料的理解，更好地保留标记信息。此外，它还有助于读者批判性地理解篇章信息，发现问题或形成自己的观点，从而提炼出有价值的信息。

- **语料库查询**：在阅读过程中遇到重点词汇、短语或句式结构时，读者可以通过查询语料库来加深对它们的理解。语料库指经科学取样和加工的大规模电子文本库，其中存放的是在实际使用中真实出现过的语言材料。相比于词典，语料库中提供的语料更具典型性、代表性和权威性。常用的英语语料库包括"英国国家语料库"（British National Corpus）和"美国当代英语语料库"（Corpus of Contemporary American English）。

- **总结提炼**：对于具有参考价值的文章，读者可以尝试进行总结和提炼，这样有利于厘清文章脉络、总结核心观点和提炼主题思想。在遇到结构内容比较复杂的语篇时，读者可以尝试创建思维导图，通过图画或图表等可视化方式厘清逻辑，从而加深理解。这些方法可以培养读者的逻辑思维和批判性思维，进而提升想象力和创造力。

Section B Translation

Text 3

The Big Bang: It Sure Was Big!

Figure 1.3 Creation of the Universe
(Source: Pixabay website)

One of the most persistently asked questions has been: How was the universe created? Many once believed that the universe had no beginning or end and was truly infinite. Through the inception of the Big Bang theory, however, no longer could the universe be considered infinite. The universe was forced to take on the properties of a finite phenomenon, possessing a history and a beginning.

We have made a first attempt at explaining the answers that science has revealed about our universe. Our understanding of the Big Bang, the first atoms, and the age of the universe is obviously incomplete. As time wears on, more discoveries are made, leading to infinite questions which require yet more answers. Unsatisfied with our base of knowledge research is being conducted around the world at this very moment to further our minimal understanding of the unimaginably complex universe.

① Since its conception, the theory of the Big Bang has been constantly challenged. ② These challenges have led those who believe in the theory to search for more concrete evidence which would prove them correct. ③ From the point at which this chapter leaves off, many have tried to go further and several discoveries have been made that paint a more complete picture of the creation of the universe.

CHAPTER 1   Mysterious Universe

④ Recently, NASA has made some astounding discoveries which lend themselves to the proof of the Big Bang theory. ⑤ Most importantly, astronomers using the Astro-2 observatory were able to confirm one of the requirements for the foundation of the universe through the Big Bang. ⑥ In June, 1995, scientists were able to detect primordial helium, such as deuterium, in the far reaches of the universe. ⑦ These findings are consistent with an important aspect of the Big Bang theory that a mixture of hydrogen and helium was created at the beginning of the universe.

⑧ In addition, the Hubble Telescope, named after the father of the Big Bang theory, has provided certain clues as to what elements were present following creation. ⑨ Astronomers using Hubble have found the element boron in extremely ancient stars. ⑩ They postulate that its presence could be either a remnant of energetic events at the birth of galaxies or it could indicate that boron is even older, dating back to the Big Bang itself. If the latter is true, scientists will be forced once again to modify their theory for the birth of the universe and events immediately afterward because, according to the present theory, such a heavy and complex atom could not have existed.

In this manner, we can see that the research will never be truly complete. Our hunger for knowledge will never be satiated. So, to answer the question, what now, is an impossibility. The path we take from here will only be determined by our own discoveries and questions. We are engaged in a never-ending cycle of questions and answers where one will inevitably lead to the other.

(Source: University of Michigan website)

Exercises

Task A Review the original translation of the underlined sentences in the source text and make any necessary revisions. Then learn how to improve your revisions from the analysis and modification of the translation provided.

这篇短文介绍了一种关于宇宙诞生的理论假设——"大爆炸"理论，全文围绕"大爆炸"理论的一系列争议、探索和发现展开。译文评析如下：

原文①②：Since its conception, the theory of the Big Bang has been constantly challenged. These challenges have led those who believe in the theory to search for more concrete evidence which would prove them correct.

初译①②：自提出以来,"大爆炸"理论就不断受到挑战。这些挑战促使那些相信这一理论的人去寻找更具体的证据来证明他们是正确的。

学生评改：

评析：原文①和②中都有 challenge 这个单词,初译将其翻译为"挑战"并不恰当。这是因为 challenge 既有"挑战"的意思,也有"质疑"的意思。通常情况下,如果对象是人的话,那么 challenge 可以译为"挑战"。例如,"Marsyas thought he could play the flute better than Apollo and challenged the god to a contest." 可以译为"马耳叙阿斯觉得他长笛吹得比阿波罗好,便向这位神发出挑战"。而如果对象是事物或理念的话,那么 challenge 通常译为"质疑"。又如,"The move was immediately challenged by two republicans." 可以译为"这项提案立即遭到了两名共和党人的质疑"。初译者在处理该词时,没有考虑其一词多义的情况,而是直接将其译为自己最熟悉的"挑战"的意思,结果造成误译。

改译："大爆炸"理论自提出以来,就不断受到质疑。这些质疑促使笃信这一理论的人们去寻找更加确凿的证据来证明其合理性。

原文③：From the point at which this chapter leaves off, many have tried to go further and several discoveries have been made that paint a more complete picture of the creation of the universe.

初译③：从本章停止的地方,许多人试图继续探索,并且已经有了几个发现,这使我们可以描绘一幅宇宙创造时更完整的画面。

学生评改：

CHAPTER **1** Mysterious Universe

> 评析： 本句的难点在于状语 From the point at which this chapter leaves off 的翻译，初译将其直译为"从本章停止的地方"，这一做法并不可取。原文中 the point 的指代并不明确，它既可能指"本章写作完成的时间点"，又可能指"本章没有涉及的内容"或"本章没有深入讨论的观点"。而直译为"从本章停止的地方"既不符合汉语的表达习惯，又容易误导读者。鉴于此，译者可以采取模糊处理的方法，译为"从本章出发……"，这样既可以避免误译，又符合汉语的表达习惯。因此在翻译过程中，译者首先要读懂原文的意思，再根据汉语的表达习惯重新组织语言，而不是采取"死译""硬译"等机械对等的方式。
>
> 改译： 从本章出发，许多人继续尝试探索并有了一些发现，这使我们可以更加完整地描绘宇宙诞生时的场景。

> 原文④： Recently, NASA has made some astounding discoveries which lend themselves to the proof of the Big Bang theory.
>
> 初译④： 最近，美国国家航空航天局有了一些惊人的发现，从而证实了"大爆炸"理论。

学生评改：_____

_____

> 评析： 原文中的 lend themselves to the proof of the Big Bang theory 被误译为"从而证实了'大爆炸'理论"。词组 lend oneself to 是指"参与"某项活动或"有助于"某事的进展或实施，此处的意思是美国国家航空航天局的一些发现为"大爆炸"理论提供了佐证，而非已经证实了"大爆炸"理论。此外，通过常识也可以很容易地识别初译中的这个逻辑错误。因为"大爆炸"理论是一个具有很大争议的假设，很少有人会断言某个或某些发现证实了该理论。因此，译者需要锻炼自己的读者意识，时常从译文中跳脱出来，重新审视自己的译文。
>
> 改译： 最近，美国国家航空航天局取得了一些惊人的发现，为"大爆炸"理论提供了一定的佐证。

原文⑤：Most importantly, astronomers using the Astro-2 observatory were able to confirm one of the requirements for the foundation of the universe through the Big Bang.

初译⑤：最重要的是，天文学家利用 Astro-2 天文台能够通过大爆炸确认宇宙产生的基础要求之一。

学生评改：_____

评析：初译⑤存在两个主要问题。第一个问题在于上下文不够连贯，主要表现在对 Most importantly 的翻译上。如果只考虑语义，将 Most importantly 译为"最重要的是"是没有问题的，但是鉴于前文已经提到"美国国家航空航天局取得了一些惊人的发现"，此处的 Most importantly 实际上是想要强调"最重要的发现"，因此直接翻译并不恰当，而是应该明确表达，以确保翻译的连贯性。另一个问题在于对 the requirements for the foundation of the universe through the Big Bang 这一短语的理解出现了偏差。初译误将 through the Big Bang 修饰的对象理解为 confirm one of the requirements，实际上该短语修饰的是 the foundation of the universe。此外，"基础要求之一"这一表述也不准确。

改译：其中最重要的发现是，通过使用 Astro-2 天文观测台，天文学家得以确认宇宙通过大爆炸产生的一个基本条件。

原文⑥：In June, 1995, scientists were able to detect primordial helium, such as deuterium, in the far reaches of the universe.

初译⑥：1995 年 6 月，科学家们能够在宇宙的远端探测到原始氦元素，如氘。

学生评改：_____

评析：初译⑥将"primordial helium, such as deuterium"译为"原始氦元素，如氘"容易引起误解。因为氘是氢的同位素，可以通过聚变反应生成氦，

CHAPTER **1** Mysterious Universe

但不能称为原始氢元素。读者虽然可能不具备这些专业知识，但在读到前后逻辑出现问题的译文时仍会感到十分费解。因此在这种情况下，译者可以选用"原初"这个词，将其译为"原初氦，如氘"；或者采取意译的方式，将二者之间的关系表述清楚，如译为"探测到可以聚变成氦的元素，如氘"。

改译：1995 年 6 月，科学家们在宇宙深处探测到可以聚变成氦的元素，如氘。

原文⑦：These findings are consistent with an important aspect of the Big Bang theory that a mixture of hydrogen and helium was created at the beginning of the universe.

初译⑦：这些发现与宇宙"大爆炸"理论的一个重要方面相符，即在宇宙诞生之初就产生了氢和氦的混合物。

学生评改：_____

_____

评析：此句翻译得较为妥当，语义准确、表达通顺。

原文⑧：In addition, the Hubble Telescope, named after the father of the Big Bang theory, has provided certain clues as to what elements were present following creation.

初译⑧：此外，以"大爆炸"理论之父的名字命名的哈勃望远镜，提供了一些宇宙诞生后元素存在的确切线索。

学生评改：_____

_____

评析：初译⑧中存在两处错误：第一处是 what elements were present 中的 what 被误省了，仅仅译为"元素存在"；另一处错误比较隐蔽，即 certain clues 应当被译为"一些线索"，而不是"确切线索"。这是因为

19

certain这个单词既有"某个""某些"的意思，也有"确切""确定"的意思，但是用法不同。当certain意为"某个""某些"时，通常用作定语形容词，如certain person（某人）、certain evidence（某些证据）；当其意为"确切""确定"时，通常用作表语形容词，如"She's absolutely certain she's going to marry a military man."（她十分确信自己将会嫁给一位军人）。此处，在certain clues这个短语中，certain明显用作定语形容词，因此应当译为"一些线索"。

改译：此外，哈勃望远镜（以"大爆炸"理论之父的名字命名）观测到的数据为宇宙诞生之后存在哪些元素提供了一些线索。

原文⑨：Astronomers using Hubble have found the element boron in extremely ancient stars.

初译⑨：天文学家使用哈勃望远镜在远古星体中发现了硼元素。

学生评改：_____

_____

评析：此句翻译得较为妥当，语义准确、表达通顺。

原文⑩：They postulate that its presence could be either a remnant of energetic events at the birth of galaxies or it could indicate that boron is even older, dating back to the Big Bang itself.

初译⑩：他们推测硼的存在可能是星系形成时超能事件的残余物，或表明硼的历史更早，可以追溯到"大爆炸"本身。

学生评改：_____

_____

评析：原文⑩中有一个明显的表示并列关系的短语either...or，但是这种并列关

CHAPTER 1　Mysterious Universe

> 系在译文中并没有充分体现出来。虽然初译⑩中使用"或"这个表示并列的连词，但是通读译文后读者很难看出前后的并列关系。如果采取直译的方法，译为"要么是星系形成时超能事件的残余物，要么表明硼的历史更早，可以追溯到'大爆炸'本身"则显得过于机械、呆板。不妨借助原文中表示可能性的 could 一词，将其译为"可能是星系诞生时能量事件的残余，也可能更早，可以追溯到'大爆炸'时期"。这样既体现了两种推测之间的并列关系，同时表述更加地道、自然。
>
> **改译**：他们推测硼元素的存在可能是星系诞生时能量事件的残余，也可能更早，可以追溯到"大爆炸"时期。

Task B Translate the following text into Chinese.

For beauty and interest alike, there are few objects in the starry heavens to compare with Saturn. This magnificent planet, with the system of rings that encircles it, provides an unforgettable spectacle when it is viewed through a powerful telescope. The Saturnian system includes not only the planet and its rings, but also 11 or more satellites, or moons.

To the ancients Saturn appeared to be the most insignificant of the heavenly bodies that were supposed to circle the Earth (the Sun, the Moon, Mercury, Venus, Mars, Jupiter, and Saturn), as distinguished from the fixed stars. The glorious rings that surround the planet were invisible before the invention of the telescope in the first decade of the 17th century. Otherwise this magnificent crown might have saved Saturn from the sinister reputation that it once bore. Ancient astrologers maintained that it had a sinister influence upon people.

Saturn is far from the center of the solar system. The mean distance of Saturn from the Sun is 1,428,000,000 kilometers, or about 9.5 times the distance of the Earth from the Sun. The density of Saturn is very low, much lower than that of any other planet. In fact, it is only about three-quarters that of water. Because of this fact, some astronomers hold that Saturn is far from having reached the solid condition.

Translation Tips 科技语篇的翻译标准

在翻译活动中,译者需要以一定的翻译标准作为指导。翻译标准既是翻译工作必须遵循的准绳,同时是衡量译文的尺度。古今中外,关于翻译标准的论述十分广泛,不少学者和翻译家都提出了自己的真知灼见。比如,美国著名翻译理论家尤金·奈达(Eugene Nida)提出的"功能对等"、清代翻译家严复的"信、达、雅",以及当代翻译家张培基倡导的"忠实、通顺"等,这些都是指导翻译活动的重要原则和标准。不过,上述翻译标准和原则大多针对文学翻译,并不完全适用于科技语篇的翻译。鉴于科技语篇独有的文体特征,译者在翻译时可以遵循以下标准或原则。

1. 准确规范

科技语篇中涉及大量专业知识和技术词汇,译者在翻译过程中必须做到准确、规范,不折不扣地传递原文的全部信息内容,并遵循专业领域特定的语言习惯和表达方式,不得任意歪曲、遗漏或增删。例如:

原文:Velocity changes if either the speed or the direction changes.
初译:如果速度或方向任何一个发生了变化,那么速率也会发生变化。
改译:如果速率或方向任何一个发生了变化,那么速度也会发生变化。

原文中的 velocity 和 speed 两个单词都有"速度"和"速率"的意思,但根据物理学知识,"速度"是一个矢量,既有大小也有方向,而"速率"是一个标量,只有大小没有方向。根据这一点,我们可以判断出初译不准确,改译的逻辑比较合理。

2. 通顺流畅

如果不考虑英汉两种语言的差异,直接将原文内容机械地转换为译文,那么极有可能会影响译文的可读性,不易被目的语读者接受。因此,译文语言必须自然流畅、逻辑清楚、文理通顺,尽量避免"死译""硬译"的情况发生。例如:

原文:With the same number of protons, all nuclei of a given element may have the different number of neutrons.
初译:具有同样数量质子的同一元素的所有原子核可能拥有不同数量的中子。
改译:对于同一元素而言,其所有原子核都具有相同数量的质子,但中子数量可能有所不同。

初译虽然基本传递了原文的意思,但却不符合汉语的表达习惯,读上去不够通顺、流畅。改译对原文结构进行了较大的重组和调整,突出了内部的逻辑关系,更加贴切和自然。

3. 简洁明晰

科技语篇的一个典型特征就是简洁明晰，因此在科技英语翻译时应尽量避免冗长、啰唆的语言表述，尽可能做到简短精练、一目了然。例如：

原文：The removal of minerals from water is called softening.
初译：将水中的矿物质去除被称为"软化"。
改译：去除水中的矿物质称为"软化"。

原文中的 The removal of minerals from water 是名词化结构做主语，汉译时可以采取词性转换的方法将 removal 转换为动词"去除"，从而将主语变为一个动宾短语，即改译中的"去除水中的矿物质"。这般修改使改译较初译而言显得更加简洁、明晰。

CHAPTER 2
Aerospace Engineering

Introduction

　　Looking up at the night sky, we may marvel at the vast and boundless universe. Each and every star is so small, but emits dazzling light like a diamond. Is there life on other planets? How far are we from going to space? Curiosity about space leads human beings to explore the unknown world. The vast sea of stars in the universe contains countless mysteries waiting for us to explore. In this chapter, Text 1 is a passage for fast reading, dealing with a space telescope; Text 2 is a passage for intensive reading, introducing a Chinese space station; and Text 3 is a passage for translation, discussing a ramjet engine. The learning objective of this chapter is to familiarize the learners with the lexical features and word translation of EST.

Lead-in Questions

1. In everyday English, "rocket science" is a common phrase denoting a difficult subject, but as a branch of the discipline, it actually refers to the astronautics branch in aerospace engineering. Do you know the foci of aerospace engineering?

2. What do you know about the principles of aeronautical engineering and astronautical engineering? Are there any overlaps between them?

Section A Fast and Intensive Reading

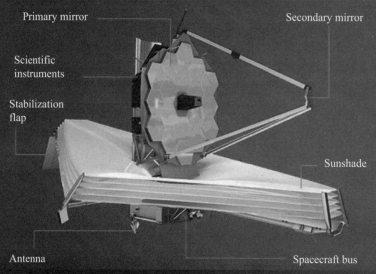

Text 1

James Webb Space Telescope

Figure 2.1　James Webb Space Telescope
(Source: The Space Techie website)

A　The biggest space observatory ever constructed will look further through space (and time) than any other telescope. The James Webb Space Telescope (JWST) has now reached its final destination. Now cooling down and deploying instruments, it won't be long until the telescope will begin reporting back with findings and exciting new imagery. The successor to the Hubble Space Telescope, NASA's new and much improved space observatory has several goals in mind for its trip into space. But what is the timeline of the JWST, how does it differ from Hubble, and who is James Webb, the man the telescope is named after? We've answered these questions and more below.

B　The James Webb Space Telescope has now reached L2 Orbit—its final destination, about 1.5 million kilometers from Earth. This is a journey that has taken roughly a month to complete. You can track its progress with NASA's "Where is Webb" feature. Not only does this show the current distance from Earth but also the telescope's speed, temperature, how long it has been in orbit, and what its next stage is.

C　The telescope was launched into space on the 24th December, 2021. While the telescope has now officially launched, it saw a huge number of delays to

CHAPTER 2 Aerospace Engineering

get to this point. The observatory was originally expected to launch back in 2007. Since then, it has experienced over 16 launch delays with the pandemic extending the date way past the last expected date of March 2021. The telescope was launched on the *Ariane 5* rocket. This is a specialized rocket which is designed to take satellites and other payloads into transfer or low-Earth orbit.

D   You might be thinking, who gets the honor of having such a historic telescope named after him or her? Well, that title goes to James Edwin Webb, the second administrator of NASA, best known for heading up Apollo—the first space program to send humans to the Moon. He was also instrumental in the two crewed space programs that followed on from Apollo: Mercury and Gemini. While Webb did eventually die in 1992, aged 85, he left a massive legacy behind, deserving of a telescope named after him.

E   "It is fitting that Hubble's successor be named in honor of James Webb. Thanks to his efforts, we got our first glimpses at the dramatic landscape of outer space," said former NASA administrator Sean O'Keefe about the observatory's name. "He took our nation on its first voyages of exploration, turning our imagination into reality." The telescope hasn't always been named after Webb. It started its life being known as the Next Generation Space Telescope which, realistically, isn't the most imaginative name we've ever heard!

F   For a long time, all of the attention was on the launch of the telescope but now that it is out of the way, we can look at what its timeline will look like. In the first month, the satellite was deploying its many components. In this stage, the telescope and instruments rapidly cooled, thanks to the sunshield, but it would take a few more weeks for them to cool to stable temperatures. At this stage, mirrors would be deployed and tests would be made to be sure they move.

G   For the next couple of months after this, the satellite will begin its tests. Using the Fine Guidance Sensor, the JWST will be pointed at a bright star to demonstrate it can acquire and lock onto targets. Then, the long process of aligning the telescope optics begins. After this, calibrations will be made on all of the scientific instrument's different modes of operation. In this stage, observations will commence, tracking moving targets like asteroids, comets, moons, and planets in our own solar system. From this point onward, Webb will begin its science mission, conducting routine tests and reporting back information.

H   Billed as the successor to the Hubble Space Telescope, the JWST is the largest space observatory ever built. Its gigantic sunshield base measures a massive 22 meter by 12 meter, roughly the same size as a tennis court. Although nearly twice as big as Hubble (which is only 13 meter long), the JWST is almost half the weight at 6,500 kg. The JWST's gold-plated mirrors have a total diameter of 6.5 meter, much larger than Hubble's 2.4-meter-diameter plate. Overall, the JWST will have approximately a 15 times wider view than Hubble.

I   Using its infrared telescope, the JWST observatory will examine objects over 13.6 billion light-years away. Because of the time it takes light to travel across the universe, this means that the JWST will effectively be looking at objects 13.6 billion years ago, an estimated 100 to 250 million years after the Big Bang. This is the furthest back in time ever observed by humanity.

J   After launching into space, the JWST will orbit the Sun, flying up to 1.5 million kilometers from Earth in temperatures reaching −223℃. For comparison, the Moon is 384,400 kilometers away, while the Hubble Space Telescope flies only 570 kilometers above our planet. As the JWST will operate so far away from Earth, it will not be able to be serviced by astronauts if any faults arise.

K   As the JWST is a product of an international collaboration between NASA, the European Space Agency (ESA), and the Canadian Space Agency (CSA), it has many mission goals. These include:

- examine the first light in the universe and the celestial objects which formed shortly after the Big Bang;
- investigate how galaxies formed and evolved;
- study the atmospheres of distant exoplanets;
- capture images of planets in our own solar system;
- locate evidence of dark matter.

L   The JWST is expected to operate for five years after its launch. However, NASA hopes the observatory will last longer than 10 years. Unfortunately, the observatory won't be able to operate forever: Although mostly solar-powered, the JWST needs a small amount of finite fuel to maintain its orbit and instruments.

(Source: Science Focus *magazine*)

CHAPTER **2** Aerospace Engineering

 **Notes**

NASA: National Aeronautics and Space Administration, a U.S. government organization that does research into space and organizes space travel 美国国家航空航天局

the Canadian Space Agency (CSA): a federal agency, established in 1989, responsible for managing all of Canada's civil space-related activities 加拿大航天局

the European Space Agency (ESA): an intergovernmental organization dedicated to the exploration of space, established in 1975 and headquartered in Paris, France, with 22 member states 欧洲航天局；欧洲太空总署

 Exercises

Task A **Identify the paragraph from which each of the following statements is derived. You may choose a paragraph more than once. Each paragraph in the above text is marked with a letter.**

1. The formal observations of the telescope won't start until several months after its launch.

2. The James Webb Space Telescope is nearly twice as big as the Hubble Space Telescope.

3. The James Webb Space Telescope was named after the second administrator of NASA.

4. Initially, the James Webb Space Telescope had another name.

5. One of the James Webb Space Telescope goals is to look for the evidence of dark matter.

6. After the launch, it would take weeks for the telescope and its instruments to cool down.

7. It took around a month for the James Webb Space Telescope to reach its final destination in space.

8. Because the James Webb Space Telescope is so far away from the Earth, it would be impossible to fix it if any faults occur.

9. The James Webb Space Telescope has experienced a lot of delays before its launch.

10. The James Webb Space Telescope can observe objects as far as 13.6 billion light-years away.

Task B Work in groups to discuss the following topic and share your opinions with the class.

Can Humans Create a Self-sustaining Community in Space?

SpaceX has proposed a plan to send humans to Mars and establish a sustainable settlement there. The goal of the settlement is to create a backup for humanity and ensure the survival of the human race in case of a catastrophic event on the Earth. Do you think this plan is feasible, given the ongoing progress in space exploration and technology? What challenges and obstacles must be overcome to make it a reality?

Text 2
China's Tiangong Space Station

Figure 2.2 Chinese Astronauts at the Tiangong Space Station
(Source: Space website)

Three astronauts on China's new space station have just performed the country's first spacewalk and are busy configuring the module for future crews. Named Tiangong ("heavenly palace"), the station is the **Chinese National Space Agency**'s (CNSA) signature project to develop China's ambitions for having humans in orbit around Earth for a long amount of time.

Chinese National Space Agency 中国国家航天局

In planning since the late 1990s, the Tiangong station's **core module**, Tianhe ("heavenly river" and an old Chinese name for the Milky Way), launched on April 29. But it isn't yet complete. Yang Liwei, chief designer of China's human spaceflight program, has said the astronauts "have a lot of tasks to do after entering the core module. For screws alone, they have over 1,000 to remove."

core module 核心舱

Much like the former Russian space station Mir and the **International Space Station**, the entire project is too large to be put into orbit with one launch. Tianhe, which weighs 22.5 tons, was lofted to an orbit of 400 km above Earth on a *Long March-5B* rocket from the Wenchang launch site on the island of Hainan, China. For context, the *Long March-5B* is a heavy-lift rocket with a thrust in between the SpaceX rockets *Falcon 9* and *Falcon Heavy*.

International Space Station 国际空间站

The core module contains everything needed to keep people alive in space. This includes: life support systems, a kitchen, sleeping and sanitation areas, electrical power management, and firefighting equipment.

To help sustain the three astronauts on their six-day working week, the kitchen is currently well-stocked with more than 120 different types of food. The core module is also equipped with **docking ports**. These will enable future modules, astronaut flights, and robotic cargo **re-supply capsules** to dock. To prepare for Tiangong, China launched two test space stations—Tiangong-1 and Tiangong-2.

docking port 连接埠

re-supply capsule 补给舱

The first of these, launched in 2011, was visited multiple times by Chinese astronauts, who tested docking procedures with cargo craft. And the station was decommissioned in 2016. Tiangong-2, launched in 2016, was a shorter-lived test station designed to assess living conditions in orbit, including growing food and measuring radiation levels. This station had a controlled descent, burning up over the Pacific Ocean in 2019.

Aside from the core module, the pressurized modules of the current Tiangong space station will consist of two laboratories, Mengtian ("heavenly dreams") and Wentian ("heavenly quest"), which will be launched over the next few years. The design of each of these laboratory modules will be based on Tiangong-2's facilities.

Unlike the International Space Station, where the bulk of electrical power to all modules is supplied by large solar arrays on purpose-built **gantries**, on Tiangong each module launched carries its own solar array. Once complete, Tiangong will weigh over 60 tons, be capable of hosting three astronauts for extended stays in space, and will have the capacity to support future spacewalks and science experiments. These can be mounted both inside

gantry（发射航天器的）塔架

CHAPTER 2 Aerospace Engineering

the pressurized modules and on deployable racks outside in space.

International collaboration is a significant part of the project. For example, astronauts from the European Space Agency trained with Chinese astronauts in ocean survival. In the event that astronauts ever had to leave an orbiting space station and return to Earth quickly, there is a high chance they would land in water and would need to survive until rescue. ESA's long-term goal with such training would be that it will one day enable its astronauts to fly aboard Chinese space missions.

More recently, nine international science experiments have been selected by CNSA for installation aboard Tiangong in the coming years. The agency received 42 applications of interest from many different countries. Of those selected, experiments include POLAR-2, a sensor designed to study the light from **gamma-ray bursts**, which are some of the most powerful explosions in the universe.

gamma-ray burst 伽马射线爆发

Another is Tumors in Space, a project lead by researchers in Norway which will look at how the microgravity and radiation environment of space affects the growth of tumors.

With another platform for humans to live in the long term in orbit, we hope that the amazing success of the International Space Station will be replicated on the Tiangong station. The experience that the astronauts gain will no doubt be invaluable for planning future lunar and Martian exploration efforts.

Recently, Russia and China unveiled a roadmap for the International Lunar Research Station. This project will involve numerous robotic lunar orbiters and landers, and will culminate in a human-crewed research facility, either in lunar orbit or on the surface. This project, if successful, could see Chinese and Russian astronauts based on the Moon from the 2030s. Tiangong is one of a number of notable successes for the Chinese space program in recent years. These include the first lunar sample-return mission since the 1970s, and the country's first robotic lander on the Martian surface, complete with rover, which successfully touched down in May this year.

In the new space race, China is clearly a real contender.

(Source: Inverse website)

Exercises

Task A **Decide whether the following statements are true (T) or false (F).**

1. Tianhe ("heavenly river") is the core module of the Tiangong space station.
2. Totally, there are two space stations in China, which are Tiangong-1 and Tiangong-2.
3. The current Tiangong space station will consist of two laboratories, Mengtian ("heavenly dreams") and Wentian ("heavenly quest").
4. Both Tiangong-1 and Tiangong-2 were designed to test docking procedures with cargo craft and assess living conditions in orbit.
5. The Tiangong-1 test space station was visited multiple times by both Chinese and Russian astronauts.

Task B **Choose the word or phrase which is closest in meaning to the underlined part in each sentence.**

1. Three astronauts on China's new space station have just performed the country's first spacewalk and are busy <u>configuring</u> the module for future crews.

    A. modifying *B.* setting up
    C. correcting *D.* transforming

2. For context, the *Long March-5B* is a heavy-lift rocket with a <u>thrust</u> in between the SpaceX rockets *Falcon 9* and *Falcon Heavy*.

    A. force *B.* pressure *C.* stimulus *D.* drive

3. Unlike the International Space Station, where the bulk of electrical power to all modules is supplied by large solar arrays on purpose-built <u>gantries</u>, on Tiangong each module launched carries its own solar array.

   A. crafts B. cranes C. frames D. signs

4. These can be mounted both inside the pressurized modules and on <u>deployable</u> racks outside in space.

   A. open B. moving C. removable D. extensible

5. With another platform for humans to live in the long term in orbit, we hope that the amazing success of the International Space Station will be <u>replicated</u> on the Tiangong station.

   A. shifted B. transported C. duplicated D. developed

Task C Answer the following questions based on the text.

1. What is the Chinese National Space Agency's ambition in building the Tiangong space station?

2. What is the difference between the International Space Station and China's Tiangong space station?

3. What is the task of Tiangong-2 launched in 2016?

4. Can you provide an example of the international collaboration of China's Tiangong space station project?

5. How do you understand the last sentence "In the new space race, China is clearly a real contender"?

Reading Tips 科技英语的词汇特点

科技英语词汇虽然只占整个篇章的 5% 到 10%，但一直都是科技语篇阅读和翻译的难点。总体而言，科技英语中的特殊词汇可以大致分为专业技术词汇（technical words）和半专业技术词汇（semi-technical words）两种。科技英语词汇的构词方式复杂，既有包含希腊语和拉丁语词缀、词根的复合词，也有很多新造词和外来语。因此，了解科技英语的词汇特征，包括构词方式、屈折变化、用词特点等，可以提高阅读科技语篇的效率。

1. 词汇分类

专业技术词汇是指用于特定学科专业的词汇和术语，这些词汇通常具有单义性、稳定性等特点。例如，antibody（[医学] 抗体）、ampere（[电学] 安培）、calculus（[数学] 微积分）、radio telescope（[天文学] 射电望远镜）等词汇分属不同的学科专业领域，而且意义十分稳定，一般不会产生歧义。

半专业技术词汇大多数由日常语言中的普通词汇转化而来，在科技语篇中的含义由其基本意义扩展衍生而来，而且在不同学科中的含义会有所不同。例如，carrier 的基本意义是指"搬运的人或工具"，但它在医学中是指"带菌者"，在军事中是指"航空母舰"，在化学中是指"载体"，在车辆制造中是指"底盘"，在机械行业中是指"托架""传导管"。这类词汇的含义十分丰富，因此必须结合具体的学科专业领域进行确定。

2. 构词方式

科技英语词汇的构词方式主要有派生（derivation）、合成（compound）和缩略（abbreviation）三种。

（1）派生

派生法是指由词根加上词缀构成新词的构词方式。很多科技英语词汇都是由希腊语或拉丁语词根加上前缀（prefix）或后缀（suffix）构成的。例如：

- anti-：表示"反抗""阻止""防止""中和"，如 anticancer（抗癌）、antibody（抗体）、anticorrosive（防腐蚀的）等。
- auto-：表示"自动的""自动调整的""自己""本身"，如 autonomy（自治）、autoignition（自燃）、automobile（汽车）等。
- -ology：表示"……学"，如 cosmology（宇宙学）、physiology（生理学）、metrology（度量衡学）等。
- proof：表示"防……的""不透……的""抗……的"，如 waterproof（防水的）、heatproof（隔热的）、shockproof（防震的）等。

CHAPTER 2　Aerospace Engineering

（2）合成

将两个词合并在一起构成一个新词的方法称为合成法。合成词可以写成单个词（如 aircraft），也可以用连字符连接（如 temperature-zone），还可以分开书写（如 sports shoes）。合成词既可以是复合名词（compound noun），也可以是复合形容词（compound adjective）。例如：

- 复合名词：battleship（战舰）、radiophotography（无线电传真）、colorimeter（色度计）、anti-armored-fighting-vehicle-missile（反装甲车导弹）、greenhouse（温室）等。
- 复合形容词：full-enclosed（全封闭的）、high-speed（高速的）、flightworthy（具备飞行条件的）、on-and-off-the-road（路面越野两用的）、general-purpose（通用的）等。

（3）缩略

在科技英语中，为了达到简洁、精练的效果，通常会大量使用缩略词。一般而言，科技英语中应用的缩略一般采用首字母缩略（initialing）、截短（clipping）和拼缀（blending）三种方法。

首字母缩略是指选取词组中每个单词的首字母来构成新词。例如：

- AI = artificial intelligence（人工智能）；CPU = central processor unit（中央处理器）；AIDS = Acquired Immune Deficiency Syndrome（艾滋病）

截短是指将一个较长的单词截短用以构成新词。例如：

- aeroplane = plane（飞机）；trigonometry = trig（三角几何）；parachute = chute（降落伞）；executive = exec（执行）

拼缀是将两个单词的某一部分合并构成新词，或者将一个单词加上另一个单词的一部分构成新词。例如：

- transceiver = transmitter + receiver（无线电收发器）；comsat = communication + satellite（通信卫星）；optocoupler = optical + coupler（光耦合器）；newscast = news + broadcast（新闻广播）

3. 复数的特殊形式

有很多科技英语的专业词汇源自拉丁语或希腊语，多以 -us、-a、-um、-on 等结尾。这些名词要注意其复数的特殊形式，例如：

- bacillus → bacilli；bacterium → bacteria；medium → media（注：也有 mediums 的形式，但意思差别较大，其表示"中号""中型""艺术创作材料""灵媒"等意思）；phenomenon → phenomena

注意，这类名词中更多的是有两种复数形式，例如：

- focus → focuses/foci；fungus → funguses/fungi；alga → algas/algae；formula → formulas/formulae；larva → lavas/larvae；spectrum → spectrums/spectra；datum → datums/data；criterion → criterions/criteria

另外，科技英语应尽量避免使用含义不清或过于笼统的词汇，尤其是形容词，如 bad、poor、good、lame、funny、foolish 等。为了体现客观性和严谨性，科技英语中的用词还比较正式，如 accordance、constitute、induce、illustrate、conversely、amend、nevertheless 等。

Section B Translation

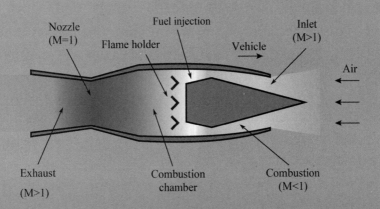

Text 3 Ramjet Engine

Figure 2.3 Schematic Diagram of Ramjet Engine
(Source: Wikipedia website)

① A ramjet, sometimes referred to as a flying stovepipe or an athodyd (aero thermodynamic duct), is a form of airbreathing jet engine that uses the engine's forward motion to compress incoming air without an axial compressor or a centrifugal compressor. ② Because ramjets cannot produce thrust at zero airspeed, they cannot move an aircraft from a standstill. ③ A ramjet-powered vehicle, therefore, requires an assisted take-off like a rocket assist to accelerate it to a speed where it begins to produce thrust.

④ Ramjets work most efficiently at supersonic speeds around Mach 3 (2,300 mph; 3,700 km/h). ⑤ This type of engine can operate up to speeds of Mach 6 (4,600 mph; 7,400 km/h). ⑥ Ramjets can be particularly useful in applications requiring a small and simple mechanism for high-speed use, such as missiles. ⑦ As speed increases, the efficiency of a ramjet starts to drop as the air temperature in the inlet increases due to compression. ⑧ As the inlet temperature gets closer to the exhaust temperature, less energy can be extracted in the form of thrust.

⑨ To produce a usable amount of thrust at yet higher speeds, the ramjet must be modified so that the incoming air is not compressed (and therefore heated) nearly as much. ⑩ This means that the air flowing through the combustion chamber is still moving very fast (relative to the engine); in fact it will be supersonic—hence the name supersonic-combustion ramjet, or scramjet.

A discussion of a ramjet engine can be simplified by assuming that the ramjet is stationary, and that air approaches the engine at a velocity equal to the vehicle speed. As air enters the inlet, adiabatic compression causes an increase in temperature and a decrease in velocity. The air is further heated by combustion of the fuel which also increases the mass flow, typically between 5% and 10%. The high-temperature compressed gases are then expanded in the nozzle and accelerated to high velocity.

The thrust developed by the engine is the net rate of change of momentum of the gases passing through the engine and is equal to the mass flow rate of the air plus burned fuel times the jet velocity minus the flow rate of air times the air velocity. The effective net thrust on the vehicle will be somewhat less than the engine thrust because of skin friction drag on the air flowing around the ramjet vehicle. There are three distinct conditions under which a ramjet engine diffuser can operate, depending on the heat released in the combustor.

When the heat released in the combustor is just enough that the back pressure at the exit section of the subsonic diffuser causes the normal shock to be positioned at the inlet throats, the operation is said to be critical; this is the design condition.

If the heat released in the combustor is increased, the static pressure at the exit of the subsonic diffuser is greater than what can be achieved under the design condition. The normal shock wave moves upstream, is expelled from the diffuser, and continues to move towards the vertex of the supersonic diffuser. Behind the normal shock wave, the flow is subsonic. Since the shock wave is detached from the inlet, the incoming air spills over the cowl of the diffuser increasing vehicle drag and possibly leading to instability.

When the heat released in the combustor is decreased, the back pressure at the outlet section of the diffusion system becomes too small to maintain the normal shock at the inlet. The excess pressure associated with the internal flow must therefore be dissipated inside the diffusion system by a strong shock wave forming in the diverging portion of the diffuser. In other words, the normal shock moves into the inlet.

(Source: Aerospace Notes website)

Exercises

Task A **Review the original translation of the underlined sentences in the source text and make any necessary revisions. Then learn how to improve your revisions from the analysis and modification of the translation provided.**

这篇短文介绍了一种适用于高空高速飞行的冲压式喷气发动机，内容涉及该发动机的工作原理和特点等。译文评析如下：

原文①：A ramjet, sometimes referred to as a flying stovepipe or an athodyd (aero thermodynamic duct), is a form of airbreathing jet engine that uses the engine's forward motion to compress incoming air without an axial compressor or a centrifugal compressor.

初译①：冲压式喷气发动机是一种吸气式喷气发动机，有时被称为冲压喷射发动机或压式喷气发动机，它没有轴向压缩机或离心压缩机，而是利用发动机的前向运动压缩空气。

学生评改：_____

_____

评析：原文①是对冲压式喷气发动机的整体介绍或界定。从语法角度看，原文①是一个包含 that 引导定语从句的复合句，可以考虑将其分为两个句子来翻译。初译的主句的翻译不够规范，导致整体的逻辑结构不清晰。这是因为插入语 sometimes referred to as a flying stovepipe or an athodyd 的处理方法不合理，其实可以将插入语放入括号中，译为"冲压式喷气发动机（也称'冲压喷射发动机'或'压式喷气发动机'）是一种吸气式喷气发动机"。这样既符合汉语的表达习惯，同时可以使句子结构更加清晰。

改译：冲压式喷气发动机（也称"冲压喷射发动机"或"压式喷气发动机"）是一种吸气式喷气发动机，它不需要使用轴流式压气机或离心式压气机，而是利用发动机的前向运动压缩空气。

原文②：Because ramjets cannot produce thrust at zero airspeed, they cannot move an aircraft from a standstill.

初译②：冲压发动机不能在零空速下产生推力，所以它们不能使飞机从静止时启动。

学生评改：_____

评析：原文②比较简单，翻译难度不大，但是需要注意术语前后的一致性。初译在翻译原文①时将 ramjet 译为"冲压式喷气发动机"，而此处却译为"冲压发动机"，显然前后不一致。虽然在专业领域里"冲压式喷气发动机"可以简称为"冲压发动机"，但是仍然不建议译者随意更换专业术语的译名。

改译：由于不能在零空速下产生推力，冲压式喷气发动机无法使飞机从静止状态启动。

原文③：A ramjet-powered vehicle, therefore, requires an assisted take-off like a rocket assist to accelerate it to a speed where it begins to produce thrust.

初译③：因此，使用冲压发动机的飞行器需要一个类似于火箭助推器的装置来辅助起飞，直至飞行器达到冲压发动机能够产生推力的速度。

学生评改：_____

评析：此句翻译除上述提到的前后术语不一致的问题之外，总体译得较为妥当，语义准确、表达通顺。

原文④⑤：Ramjets work most efficiently at supersonic speeds around Mach 3 (2,300 mph; 3,700 km/h). This type of engine can operate up to speeds of Mach 6 (4,600 mph; 7,400 km/h).

CHAPTER 2　Aerospace Engineering

初译④⑤：冲压发动机在 3 马赫（2 300 英里每小时；3 700 km/h）时达到最高效率，在 6 马赫（4 600 英里每小时；7 400 km/h）时达到速度上限。

学生评改：_____

_____

_____

评析：原文④和⑤的联系非常紧密，可以合并为一句话来翻译。初译整体上没有问题，但在速度单位的表达上不够规范：首先，速度单位的翻译需要保持统一，不能其中一个转换为汉语，另一个还保留英语；其次，速度是一个复合单位，汉语格式需要在时间单位和距离单位之间加 /。

改译：冲压式喷气发动机在 3 马赫（2 300 英里 / 小时；3 700 公里 / 小时）时达到最高效率，在 6 马赫（4 600 英里 / 小时；7 400 公里 / 小时）时达到速度上限。

原文⑥：Ramjets can be particularly useful in applications requiring a small and simple mechanism for high-speed use, such as missiles.

初译⑥：有的高速飞行器，比如导弹，需要体积小、结构简单的推力装置，冲压发动机恰好满足了这种需求。

学生评改：_____

_____

评析：初译⑥和初译①的问题类似，即译文表达冗余啰唆，不符合汉语的表达习惯。如果将译文列举的内容放到括号中，那么这个句子读上去会更加通顺、自然。

改译：某些高速飞行器（如导弹）需要体积小、结构简单的推力装置，而冲压式喷气发动机恰好满足了这种需求。

原文⑦⑧：As speed increases, the efficiency of a ramjet starts to drop as the air temperature in the inlet increases due to compression. As the inlet temperature gets closer to the exhaust temperature, less energy can be extracted in the form of thrust.

初译⑦⑧：随着来流速度变快，入口空气被压缩后的温度升高，发动机的效率就会降低。当进气温度越接近排气温度时，转化为推力形式的能量就越少。

学生评改：_____

评析：原文⑦和⑧之间的关系非常紧密，可以合并为一句话来翻译。原文⑦指出"入口处的空气温度升高会造成发动机效率降低"，但并没有给出原因，而第⑧句实际上可以看作对前一句的解释说明。因此可以将第⑧句译为原因状语从句，那么前一句"发动机效率降低"的原因就明确了。

改译：随着速度变快，入口处的空气温度会随着空气压缩而升高，发动机的效率也会降低，因为入口温度越接近出口温度，转化为推力形式的能量就越少。

原文⑨⑩：To produce a usable amount of thrust at yet higher speeds, the ramjet must be modified so that the incoming air is not compressed (and therefore heated) nearly as much. This means that the air flowing through the combustion chamber is still moving very fast (relative to the engine); in fact it will be supersonic—hence the name supersonic-combustion ramjet, or scramjet.

初译⑨⑩：为了在更高的速度下产生足够的推力，必须改进冲压发动机，以降低来流空气的压缩程度（从而减少升温）。这就意味着流经燃烧室的气流速度仍然很快（相对于普通发动机而言），可达超音速，因此被称为"超音速燃烧冲压喷气发动机"，即超燃冲压发动机。

CHAPTER 2　Aerospace Engineering

学生评改：_____

_____

_____

_____

> **评析**：原文⑨和⑩进一步介绍冲压式喷气发动机的工作原理。其中，第⑨句的翻译基本没有什么问题。第⑩句中的 relative to the engine 想要强调的是"空气相对于发动机的流速"，与发动机的类型没有关系。因此，初译中的"相对于普通发动机而言"与原文意思不符，应当修改为"相对于发动机"。
>
> **改译**：为了在高速运行的情况下产生足够的推力，必须改进冲压式喷气发动机，通过降低来流空气的压缩程度来减少温度的升高。这意味着流经燃烧室的气流速度仍然很快（相对于发动机），可达超音速。因此，这种发动机也被称为"超音速燃烧冲压式喷气发动机"，即超燃冲压式发动机。

Task B Translate the following text into Chinese.

On the brink of a new year, NASA's Hubble Space Telescope snapped a swirling mass of star dust and gas, known as spiral galaxy ESO 021-G004, and the resulting image is so gob-smacking that it's an instant reminder of how tiny and fragile our home really is.

Following its halo of illuminated cosmic matter, this neighboring galaxy draws the eye inward towards a supermassive black hole lurking within. While most black holes are quiet and invisible, this one is wide awake, and scientists say its insatiable appetite is what makes the galaxy's center burn so bright.

As cosmic material falls back into the hole, pulled by gravity, it is dragged into orbit, superheated, and eventually devoured, emitting a ton of high-energy radiation in the process. This is what's known as an active galactic nucleus, and some consider it the strongest proof for the existence of supermassive black holes.

Lucky for us, ESO 021-G004 resides a relatively nearby 130 million light-years away, in the small southern constellation of Chamaeleon, which makes it easier for us to keep our eyes on.

Translation Tips 词义的选择与引申

英汉两种语言中普遍存在一词多义、一词多类的现象，这导致两种语言在词汇层面呈现出复杂的对应情况，比如词汇不对应、部分对应、交叉对应等。另外，很多时候，词典释义并不完全符合当前的使用语境，如果译者生搬硬套、牵强附会，则可能会出现误译、错译的情况，导致译文质量下降。因此，在从事科技英语翻译时，译者需要对词义进行正确选择和适当引申。

1. 词义的选择

在科技英语翻译中，译者可以根据词类、学科专业和搭配习惯来选择和确定词义。

（1）根据词类选择词义

一般情况下，兼类词的词性不同，词义也不同。为了选择正确的词义，译者首先需要明确该词在句中承担的成分，再根据其词类选择适当的词义。例如：

原文：**Like** charges repel, **unlike** charges attract.
译文：同性电荷相斥，异性电荷相吸。

在英语中，like 是个兼类词，它可以作为动词，表示"喜欢""喜爱"；也可以作为介词，表示"像""如同"；还可以作为形容词，表示"相似的""类似的"。通过语法分析可以看出，例子中的 repel 和 attract 是动词，充当句子的谓语，而 like 和 unlike 作为形容词修饰限定 charges，因此可以分别译为"同性"和"异性"。

（2）根据学科专业选择词义

同一词汇在不同学科专业领域里可能会有不同的意义。比如 charge 这个单词用作动词时，其在不同学科专业领域里的意义差别较大。在物理学领域，它表示"充电"；在司法领域表示"指控"；在金融领域表示"收费"；而在军事学领域表示"冲锋"。因此在确定词义时，译者需要先明确词汇所属的学科专业，之后再做出选择。

（3）根据搭配习惯选择词义

在英语定语和中心词的搭配中，同一定语搭配不同的中心词时，其意义会大不相同，因此汉译时需要符合汉语的搭配习惯进行翻译。下面以英语单词 low 的翻译为例：

- **low** shot：仰视拍摄
- **low** current：低强度电流
- **low** brake：低速制动器
- **low** key：低音调键
- **low** access：慢速存取
- **low** damping：弱阻尼

2. 词义的引申

词义的引申是指从词汇的基本词义出发，结合具体语境和上下文逻辑关系加以拓展、转换或延伸，使词汇意义更加准确和地道。一般而言，词义的引申可以分为具体化引申和概括化引申两种。

（1）具体化引申

当原文中的英语词汇或短语表达过于抽象或模糊时，译者需要将其引申为表意更为具体的汉语词汇。例如：

原文：The pupil of the eye **responds to** the changes of light intensity.
译文：瞳孔可以随着光线的强弱变化而扩大或缩小。

本例中的英语短语 respond to 在词典中的释义为"对……做出反应"，如果将其直译为"瞳孔可以随着光线的强弱变化而做出反应"，读者仍然无法知晓瞳孔会做出什么反应。因此，此处宜根据语境将其具体引申为"扩大或缩小"，这样语义表达就更为准确、贴切了。

（2）概括化引申

概括化引申是指用含义概括、笼统或抽象的词汇来表达某些具体化或形象化的词汇。例如：

原文：These gases **trap** the heat of the sun, whereas sulphur dioxide cools the atmosphere.
译文：这些气体留住了阳光中的热量，而二氧化硫使空气冷却。

本例中 trap 一词用作动词，常用的词典释义是"用捕捉器捕捉""抓捕"等，用在此处十分形象具体。如果将其直译为"捕捉／抓捕了阳光中的热量"，则不符合汉语的表达习惯。改用含义更为抽象、笼统的词汇，如本例中使用的"留住"，则让译文更加通顺、自然。

CHAPTER 3
Physical Science

Introduction

Physical science is ordinarily thought of as consisting of four broad areas: astronomy, physics, chemistry, and Earth sciences. Each of these is in turn divided into fields and subfields. In its modern sense, physics was founded in the mid-19th century as a synthesis of several older sciences—mechanics, optics, acoustics, electricity, magnetism, heat, and physical properties of matter. It is a branch of natural sciences that studies non-living (or inorganic) systems, in contrast to life sciences. In this chapter, Text 1 is a passage for fast reading, introducing the functions of maglev trains; Text 2 is a passage for intensive reading, talking about the general theory of relativity; and Text 3 is a passage for translation, discussing the echo-location in bats. The learning objective of this chapter is to familiarize the learners with math expressions for EST in reading and translation.

Lead-in Questions

1. The Greek view of physics dominated science for almost 2,000 years. Do you know anything about Greek physics?
2. "General relativity is expressed in a set of interlinked differential equations that define how the shape of space-time depends on the amount of matter (or, equivalently, energy) in the region." How do you interpret this statement?

Section A Fast and Intensive Reading

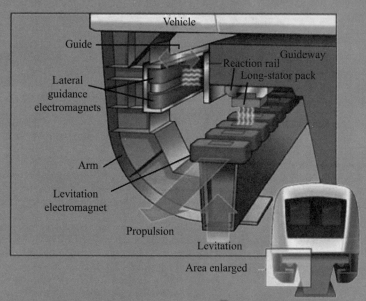

Text 1 How Maglev Trains Work

Figure 3.1   Magnetic Levitation System of Maglev Trains
(Source: ResearchGate website)

A   The evolution of mass transportation has fundamentally shifted human civilization. In the 1860s, a transcontinental railroad turned the months-long slog across America into a week-long journey. Just a few decades later, passenger automobiles made it possible to bounce across the countryside much faster than on horseback. And of course, during the World War I era, the first commercial flights began transforming our travels all over again, making coast-to-coast journeys a matter of hours. But rail trips in the U.S. aren't much faster today than they were a century ago. For engineers looking for the next big breakthrough, perhaps "magical" floating trains are just the tickets. Maglev trains (magnetically levitated train) use powerful electromagnets to develop high speed. These trains float over guideways using the basic principles of magnets to replace the old steel wheel and track trains. There's no rail friction to speak of, meaning these trains can hit speeds of hundreds of miles per hour.

B   Yet high speed is just one major benefit of maglev trains. Because the trains rarely (if ever) touch the track, there's far less noise and vibration than typical, earth-shaking trains. Less vibration and friction results in fewer mechanical

CHAPTER 3 Physical Science

breakdowns, meaning that maglev trains are less likely to encounter weather-related delays.

C   The first patents for magnetic levitation (maglev) technologies were filed by French-born American engineer Emile Bachelet all the way back in the early 1910s. Even before that, in 1904, American professor and inventor Robert Goddard had written a paper outlining the idea of maglev levitation. It wasn't long before engineers began planning train systems based on this futuristic vision. Soon, they believed, passengers would board magnetically propelled cars and zip from place to place at high speed, and without many of the maintenance and safety concerns of traditional railroads.

D   The big difference between a maglev train and a conventional train is that maglev trains do not have an engine—at least not the kind of engine used to pull typical train cars along steel tracks. The engine for maglev trains is rather inconspicuous. Instead of using fossil fuels, the magnetic field created by the electrified coils in the guideway walls and the track combine to propel the train.

E   If you've ever played with magnets, you know that opposite poles attract and like poles repel each other. This is the basic principle behind electromagnetic propulsion. Electromagnets are similar to other magnets in that they attract metal objects, but the magnetic pull is temporary. You can easily create a small electromagnet yourself by connecting the ends of a copper wire to the positive and negative ends of an AA, C or D-cell battery. This creates a small magnetic field. If you disconnect either end of the wire from the battery, the magnetic field is taken away.

F   The magnetic field created in this wire-and-battery experiment is the simple idea behind a maglev train rail system. There are three components to this system:

- a large electrical power source;
- metal coils lining a guideway or track;
- large guidance magnets attached to the underside of the train.

G   The maglev track allows the train to float above the track through the use of repelling magnets. The magnetized coil running along the track, called a guideway, repels the large magnets on the train's undercarriage, allowing the train to levitate between 0.39 and 3.93 inches (1 to 10 centimeters) above the

guideway. Once the train is levitated, power is supplied to the coils within the guideway walls to create a unique system of magnetic fields that pull and push the train along the guideway. The electric current supplied to the coils in the guideway walls is constantly alternating to change the polarity of the magnetized coils. This change in polarity causes the magnetic field in front of the train to pull the vehicle forward, while the magnetic field behind the train adds more forward thrust.

H   Maglev trains float on a cushion of air, eliminating friction. This lack of friction and the trains' aerodynamic designs allow these trains to reach unprecedented ground transportation speeds of more than 310 mph (500 kph), or twice as fast as Amtrak's fastest commuter train. In comparison, a Boeing-777 commercial airplane used for long-range flights can reach a top speed of about 562 mph (905 kph). Developers say that maglev trains will eventually link cities that are up to 1,000 miles (1,609 kilometers) apart. At 310 mph, you could travel from Paris to Rome in just over two hours. Some maglev trains are capable of even greater speeds. In October 2016, a Japan Railway maglev bullet train blazed all the way to 374 mph (601 kph) during a short run. Those kinds of speeds give engineers hope that the technology will prove useful for routes that are hundreds of miles long.

I   While maglev transportation was first proposed more than a century ago, the first commercial maglev train didn't become a reality until 1984, when a low-speed maglev shuttle became operational between the United Kingdom's Birmingham International Railway Station and an airport terminal of Birmingham International Airport. Since then, various maglev projects have started, stalled, or been outright abandoned.

J   The fact that maglev systems are fast, smooth, and efficient doesn't change one crippling fact—these systems are incredibly expensive to build. U.S. cities from Los Angeles to Pittsburgh to San Diego had maglev line plans in the works, but the expense of building a maglev transportation system (roughly $50 million to $200 million per mile) has been prohibitive and eventually killed off most of the proposed projects. Some critics lambast maglev projects as costs are perhaps five times as much as traditional rail lines. But proponents point out that the cost of operating these trains is, in some cases, up to 70% less than with old-school train technology.

CHAPTER 3　Physical Science

K　It's impossible to know exactly how maglevs will figure into the future of human transportation. Advances in self-driving cars and air travel may complicate the deployment of maglev lines. If the hyperloop industry manages to generate momentum, it could disrupt all sorts of transportation systems. And some engineers suspect that even flying cars, though incredibly pricey, might trump rail systems in the future because they don't need massive infrastructure projects to get off the ground.

(Source: HowStuffWorks website)

Notes

AA, C or D battery: typical non-lithium cylindrical cell dry batteries in the most common sizes　五号、二号或一号电池

electromagnetic propulsion: Electromagnetic propulsion (EMP) is the principle of accelerating an object by the utilization of a flowing electrical current and magnetic fields. The electrical current is used to either create an opposing magnetic field, or to charge a fluid, which can then be repelled.　电磁推力

hyperloop industry: a conceptual high-speed transportation system originally put forward by entrepreneur Elon Musk, incorporating reduced-pressure tubes in which pressurized capsules ride on an air cushion driven by linear induction motors and air compressors　超级高铁行业

lambast: to attack or criticize sb./sth. very severely, especially in public （尤指公开地）猛烈抨击，狠狠批评

Exercises

Task A **Identify the paragraph from which each of the following statements is derived. You may choose a paragraph more than once. Each paragraph in the above text is marked with a letter.**

1. The basic principle behind electromagnetic propulsion is that opposite poles attract and like poles repel each other.

2. The earliest patents related to maglev technologies can be traced back to the 1910s.

3. In America, the first commercial flights began during World War I.

4. It is unclear about the future development of maglev trains.

5. The speed of maglev trains can reach more than 600 kph.

6. The cost of building maglev systems may be five times as much as traditional rail lines.

7. Maglev trains do not have conventional train engines.

8. The train can levitate between 1 to 10 centimeters above the guideway due to the use of repelling magnets.

9. The first commercial maglev train didn't come into being until 1984.

10. Maglev trains are less affected by bad weather than traditional trains.

Task B Work in groups to discuss the following topic and share your opinions with the class.

How to Increase the Adoption of Maglev Trains?

What are the factors that have hindered the widespread adoption and development of maglev train technology globally, despite it being in existence for many years? Can you think of any potential solutions or alternative approaches to addressing these issues and promoting the application of maglev trains in transportation systems?

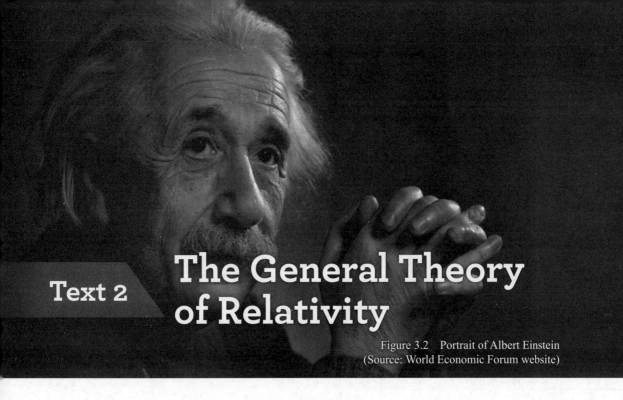

Text 2 The General Theory of Relativity

Figure 3.2 Portrait of Albert Einstein
(Source: World Economic Forum website)

The **general theory of relativity** is, as the name indicates, a generalization of the special theory of relativity. It is certainly one of the most remarkable achievements of science to date, and it was developed by Einstein with little or no experimental motivation but driven instead by philosophical questions: Why are **inertial frames of reference** so special? Why is it we do not feel gravity's pull when we are freely falling? Why should **absolute velocities** be forbidden but **absolute accelerations** be accepted?

In 1907, only two years after the publication of his special theory of relativity, Einstein wrote a paper attempting to modify Newton's theory of gravitation to fit special relativity. Was this modification necessary? Most emphatically yes! The reason lies at the heart of the special theory of relativity: Newton's expression for the **gravitational force** between two objects depends on the masses and on the distance separating the bodies, but makes no mention of time at all. In this view of the world, if one mass is moved, the other perceives the change (as a decrease or increase of the gravitational force) instantaneously. If exactly true, this would be a physical effect which travels faster than light (in fact,

general theory of relativity
广义相对论

inertial frame of reference
惯性系

absolute velocity 绝对速度
absolute acceleration 绝对加速度

gravitational force 万有引力，地心引力

at infinite speed), and would be inconsistent with the special theory of relativity. The only way out of this problem is by concluding that Newton's gravitational equations are not strictly correct. As in previous occasions this does not imply that they are "wrong", it only means that they are not accurate under certain circumstances: Situations where large velocities (and, as we will see, large masses) are involved cannot be described accurately by these equations.

In 1920, Einstein commented that a thought came into his mind when writing the above-mentioned paper. He called it "the happiest thought of my life":

The gravitational field has only a relative existence... Because for an observer freely falling from the roof of a house—at least in his immediate surroundings—there exists no gravitational field.

Let's imagine the unfortunate Wile E. Coyote falling from an immense height. As he starts falling, he lets go of the bomb he was about to drop on the Road Runner way below. The bomb does not gain on Wile nor does it lag behind. If he were to push the bomb away, he would see it move with a constant speed in a fixed direction. This realization is important because this is exactly what an astronaut would experience in outer space, far away from all bodies (we have good evidence for this: The *Apollo 10–13* spacecrafts did travel far from Earth into regions where the gravitational forces are quite weak).

Mr. Coyote is fated to repeat the experience with many other things: rocks, magnets, harpoons, anvils, etc. In all cases the same results are obtained: With respect to him all objects, irrespective of composition, mass, etc., behave as if in free space. So, if he should fall inside a closed box, he would not be able to tell whether he was plunging to his death (or, at least, severe discomfort), or

CHAPTER 3 Physical Science

whether he was in outer space on his way to Pluto at a constant speed.

This is reminiscent of Galileo's argument: The observer lets go of some objects which remain in a state of uniform motion (with respect to him!).

This behavior is independent of their chemical or physical nature (as above, air resistance is ignored). The observer (Wile), as long as he confines his observations to his immediate vicinity (that is, as long as he does not look down), has the right to interpret his state as "at rest". Just as Galileo argued that experiments in a closed box cannot determine the state of uniform motion of the box, Einstein argued that experiments in a freely falling small closed box cannot be used to determine whether the box is in the grip of a gravitational force or not.

Why would this be true? The answer can be traced back to the way in which gravity affects bodies. Remember that the quantity we called m (the mass) played two different roles in Newton's equations. One is to determine, given a force, what the acceleration of the body would be: $F = ma$ (the **inertial mass**). The other is to determine the intensity with which the said body experiences a gravitational force: $F = mMG/r^2$ (the **gravitational mass**). As mentioned before, these two quantities need not to be equal: The first "job" of m is to tell a body how much to accelerate given any force, a kick, an electric force (should the body be charged), etc. The second "job" tells the body how much of the gravitational force it should experience and also determines how strong a gravitational force it generates. But, in fact, both numbers are equal (to a precision of ten parts per billion).

inertial mass 惯性质量

gravitational mass 引力质量

What does this imply? Well, from Newton's equations we get $\dfrac{mMG}{r^2} = ma$ so that $\dfrac{MG}{r^2} = a$; this equation determines how a body moves, which trajectory it follows, how long does it take to move from one position to another, etc.! Two bodies of different masses, composition, origin, and guise will follow the same trajectory: Beans, bats, and boulders will move in the same way.

So the equality of the two m's was upgraded by Einstein to a postulate: the principle of equivalence; this one statement (that the m in ma and the m in mMG/r^2 are identical) implies an incredible amount of new and surprising effects. The m in $F = ma$ is called the inertial mass and the m in $F = mMG/r^2$ is called the gravitational mass. Then, the principle of equivalence states that the inertial and gravitational masses are identical.

The whole of the general theory of relativity rests on this postulate, and will fail if one can find a material for which the inertial and gravitational masses have different values. One might think that this represents a defect of the theory, its **Achilles heel**. In one sense, this is true since a single experiment has the potential of demolishing the whole of the theory (people have tried hard, but all experiments have validated the principle of equivalence).

On the other hand, one can argue that a theory which is based on a minimum of postulates is a better theory (since there are less assumptions involved in its construction); from this point of view, the general theory of relativity is a gem.

(Source: Trapped Ion Quantum Information at the University of Maryland website)

Achilles heel 阿喀琉斯之踵；致命要害

CHAPTER 3 Physical Science

 Exercises

***Task A** Decide whether the following statements are true (T) or false (F).*

1. The general theory of relativity was developed by Einstein with many experiments.

2. Newton's gravitational equations are not wrong but inaccurate under certain circumstances.

3. If a person should fall inside a closed box, he could not determine the state of uniform motion of the box.

4. According to Newton's equations, objects of different masses and compositions would move in different ways.

5. The Achilles heel of the general theory of relativity is that it will fail if one can find a material for which the inertial and gravitational masses have different values.

***Task B** Choose the word or phrase which is closest in meaning to the underlined part in each sentence.*

1. ...and it was developed by Einstein with little or no experimental motivation but <u>driven</u> instead by philosophical questions...
   A. ridden   *B.* run   *C.* prompted   *D.* indicated

2. In 1907, only two years after the publication of his special theory of relativity, Einstein wrote a paper attempting to <u>modify</u> Newton's theory of gravitation to fit special relativity.
   A. change   *B.* improve   *C.* correct   *D.* design

3. In this view of the world, if one mass is moved, the other perceives the change (as a decrease or increase of the gravitational force) <u>instantaneously</u>.
   A. previously   *B.* immediately   *C.* consequently   *D.* slowly

4. If exactly true, this would be a physical effect which travels faster than light (in fact, at infinite speed), and would be <u>inconsistent with</u> the special theory of relativity.
   A. false with   *B.* wrong with   *C.* different from   *D.* contradicting

5. This is <u>reminiscent</u> of Galileo's argument: The observer lets go of some objects which remain in a state of uniform motion (with respect to him!).
   A. reminding   *B.* similar   *C.* true   *D.* thinking

59

Task C Answer the following questions based on the text.

1. Why did Einstein modify Newton's theory of gravitation?
2. Under what situations does Newton's theory of gravitation not hold true?
3. What is Einstein's "the happiest thought of my life"?
4. What are the two different roles played by *m* (the mass) in Newton's equations?
5. What is the postulate on which the whole of the general theory of relativity rests?

Shanghai Transrapid

Reading Tips 科技英语中的数字用法

数字在科技语篇中的作用举足轻重。英汉两种语言在数字表达习惯上的差异很大，因此经常造成误解。比如，英语的数字位置比较灵活，可以直接做主语、表语、宾语和定语等，而汉语中的数字经常要加上量词等才可以成为句子成分。

 1. 数字的进位和倍数

汉语数字和英语数字最大的不同在于进位的表达方式。虽然都是从右边个位数数起，但英语是三位一进，汉语是四位一进，所以汉语中的"万"字是较常用的单位词，英语中常用的单位词是第一个逗号前的 thousand 和第二个逗号前的 million。因为汉英的进位不对应，翻译数字时需要进行必要的换算，并特别注意换算的准确性。

关于倍数的概念，英语中表示倍数的形式和用词较多，如 times、factor、double、triple 等。而汉语中的表达方式一般比较固定，一是增加了多少倍，二是增加到原数的多少倍。需要注意的是英汉倍数概念的区别：英语的倍数概念一般包含原基数，而汉语中一般分为包含和不包含两种情况——包含的情况表示"增加到（为）……倍"，不包含的情况则表达为"增加了……倍"。具体可见本单元 Translation Tips 部分的知识讲解。

 2. 百分数和分数

英语中百分数的表示方法比较灵活，可以是"百分数 + 形容词比较级 + than"的形式，也可以是"动词 + by/to + 百分数"的形式，但要注意英语中的增减是指净增减部分，不含底数，理解时需要根据情况灵活处理。例如：

- N% more/less than...：比……增加 / 减少了 N%
- N% higher/lower than...：比……高出 / 低了 N%
- increase/decrease by N%；grow/reduce by N%：增加 / 减少了 N%（by 表示净增减值）
- increase/decrease to N%；grow/fall to N%：增加 / 减少到 N%（to 表示净增减值）

另外，关于分数表达，在英语中一般分子用基数词表示，分母用复数的序数词表示，但有些特殊情况除外，如 $\frac{1}{2}$ 不说 one second，而说 one half 或 a half；$1\frac{1}{2}$ 读作 one and a half；比较复杂的分数，如 $\frac{45}{235}$ 读作 45 over / out of / in 235，$46\frac{123}{456}$ 读作 46 and 123 over 456（注意这类数字的分子和分母都读作基数词）。

3. 概数

英语中关于概数的固定表达方式有很多，使用时需要注意介词的正确搭配以及介词 of 前的名词复数问题。例如：

- by halves：不完全；不完整的；虎头蛇尾的（用于否定句）
- by twos and threes：三三两两
- a few tenths of：十分之几；有几成
- nine cased out of ten：十之八九
- tens/decades of：数十个
- a score of：二十
- scores of：许多；大量
- a thousand and one：无数的
- tens of thousands of：好几万的
- hundreds of thousands of：几十万的；无数的
- thousands upon thousands of：成千上万的
- hundreds of millions of：亿万的
- millions upon millions of：千百万的；数以百万计的

英语中有一些词可以表示"大约""近似""将近"等概念，常用的有 about、around、somewhere about、nearly、approximately、some、on the border of、or so、roughly 等，例如：

- **somewhere about** 2,000 meters
- One liter is **roughly** equal to one quart.

另外，还应注意表示"多于""高于""以上"等概念的常用词或词组，如 over、above、long、exceed、in excess of、odd（通常数字紧跟在后面）等；以及表示"不足""不到""以下"等相反意义的常用词或词组，如 below、off、to、less than、short of、under、as few as、no more than 等。例如：

- He has worked there for twenty-**odd** years.（他在那里工作了二十多年。）
- It has been tested for ten **long** years.（已经测试了十多年了。）
- traveling at speeds **in excess of** 100 mph（以每小时 100 多英里的速度行驶）
- **under** 20 years old（不到 20 岁）
- He was 76 votes **short of** the quota.（他比规定当选票数少了 76 票。）
- All things are 20% **off** the original number.（所有的东西都比原数少了 20%。）

Section B Translation

Text 3

The Echo-location in Bats

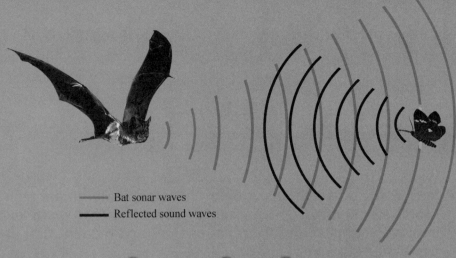

Figure 3.3 Bats Use Eco-location to Find Prey
(Source: Science Learning Hub website)

    Not all sounds made by animals serve as language, and we have only to turn to that extraordinary discovery of echo-location in bats to see a case in which the voice plays a strictly utilitarian role.

    ① To get a full appreciation of what this means we must turn first to some recent human inventions. ② Everyone knows that if he shouts in the vicinity of a wall or a mountainside, an echo will come back. ③ The further off this solid obstruction, the longer time will elapse for the return of the echo. ④ A sound made by tapping on the hull of a ship will be reflected from the sea bottom, and by measuring the time interval between the taps and the receipt of the echoes, the depth of the sea at that point can be calculated. ⑤ So was born the echo-sounding apparatus, now in general use in ships.

    ⑥ Every solid object will reflect a sound, varying according to the size and nature of the object. ⑦ A shoal of fish will do this. ⑧ So it is a comparatively simple step from locating the sea bottom to locating a shoal of fish. ⑨ With experience and with improved apparatus, it is now possible not only to locate a shoal but to tell if it is herring, cod, or other well-known fish, by the pattern of its echo.

    It has been found that certain bats emit squeaks and by receiving the echoes, they can locate and steer clear of obstacles—or locate flying insects on which they feed. This echo-location in bats is often compared with radar, the principle of which is similar.

(Source: Doubtnut website)

Exercises

Task A Review the original translation of the underlined sentences in the source text and make any necessary revisions. Then learn how to improve your revisions from the analysis and modification of the translation provided.

这篇科普短文主要讨论了蝙蝠的回声定位系统,并对其原理进行了详细的介绍。原文包括四个段落,其中第二段和第三段重点介绍了回声定位的原理,译文评析如下:

原文①:To get a full appreciation of what this means we must turn first to some recent human inventions.

初译①:要充分理解这一点,必须首先回顾一下人类近期的一些发明创造。

学生评改:_____
_____

评析:此句翻译得较为妥当,语义准确、表达通顺。

原文②:Everyone knows that if he shouts in the vicinity of a wall or a mountainside, an echo will come back.

初译②:每个人都知道如果他冲着墙或者山谷附近大喊,回声会返回。

学生评改:_____
_____

CHAPTER 3 Physical Science

评析：原文②的句子结构比较简单，意思也十分明确，但是初译②采取了机械直译的方法，结果导致翻译效果并不理想。首先，最主要的问题在于代词"他"指代不明。在原文中，代词 he 指代句首的 Everyone，用作泛指；但在汉语中，代词"他"只能用作特指，不能指代"每个人"。因此，此处的 he 最好翻译为具有泛指意义的"有人"，句首的 Everyone 相应地译为"众所周知"，这样就可以实现前后文的照应和连贯了。其次，shouts in the vicinity of a wall or a mountainside 指的是"在墙边或山坡附近大喊"，而非"冲着墙或者山谷附近大喊"，这属于典型的概念意义偏离。

改译：众所周知，如果有人在墙边或山坡附近大喊，声音就会返回来。

原文③：The further off this solid obstruction, the longer time will elapse for the return of the echo.

译文③：距离固体障碍物越远，声音返回所需的时间就越长。

学生评改：_____
_____

评析：此句翻译得较为妥当，语义准确、表达通顺。

原文④⑤：A sound made by tapping on the hull of a ship will be reflected from the sea bottom, and by measuring the time interval between the taps and the receipt of the echoes, the depth of the sea at that point can be calculated. So was born the echo-sounding apparatus, now in general use in ships.

初译④⑤：敲打船体发出的声音会从海底反射回来，通过测量敲打和接收回声之间的时间间隔，就可以计算出海洋深度。现在船舶上普遍使用的回声探测仪就是这样产生的。

学生评改: _____

_____

_____

_____

评析: 从单个句子的翻译来看,初译④和⑤都没有问题。但是如果把两个句子联系起来看,就会发现此处存在严重的逻辑不通问题。原文④主要介绍了回声探测的原理,如果把原文⑤直接译为"回声探测仪就是这样产生的",那么读者就会疑惑回声探测仪究竟是"如何"产生的。尽管大多数读者可以根据上下文推测出前后的逻辑对应关系,但是从翻译的角度来看,初译④和⑤是不成功的,因为读者需要付出较多的认知努力才能读懂原文。因此,在翻译原文⑤时应当采取"显化"的翻译策略,即把原文中隐含的信息明晰化,以实现更好的交际效果。

改译: 同样,敲打船体发出的声音会从海底反射回来,通过测量敲打和接收回声之间的时间间隔,可以计算出该处的海洋深度。目前,在船舶上广泛使用的回声探测仪就是根据该原理发明出来的。

原文⑥: Every solid object will reflect a sound, varying according to the size and nature of the object.

初译⑥: 每种固体都会反射一种声音,这种声音随物体的大小和性质变化。

学生评改: _____

_____

评析: 由于英汉两种语言的表达方式不同,如果硬把英语句子中的某些词语译成汉语,则会使译文晦涩难懂,甚至出现错误。为使译文通顺并准确地表达出原文的内容,有时需将一些词语省略不译。例如,原文⑥中的 a sound 被机械地翻译成"一种声音",这会产生歧义,误导读者认为每种固体都会反射同一种声音或者每种固体都仅能反射一种声音。实际上,这里的不定冠词 a 与单数名词 sound 连用表示泛指,翻译时可以直接将冠词省略。另外,句首的限定词 Every 也没有必要翻译出来,而是可以直接省略。省略后的译文"所有固体都可以反射声音"传递的信息不仅没有缺失，反而显得精练。

改译：所有固体都可以反射声音，回声会随着固体的大小和性质不同而有所变化。

原文⑦：A shoal of fish will do this.

初译⑦：鱼群也会这样做。

学生评改：

评析：初译⑦过于直译，结果导致译文接受性较差。通过阅读上文，读者不难理解这句话的意思，即鱼群也会反射声音，而且声音会随着鱼群种类的不同而变化。原文⑦可以完美地表达这一意思，但是直译为"鱼群也会这样做"会让人误解为鱼群会主动地反射声音，而这事实上是不可能的。其中的关键问题在于英语动词 do 是个万能词，它不仅有"做事情"的意思，还可以表达"行动""表现""执行""处理"等诸多意思。在这里，它其实表示的是"具有某种功能或属性"的意思，因此可以将其模糊化，译为"鱼群也不例外"或者"鱼群亦是如此"。

改译：鱼群亦是如此。

原文⑧：So it is a comparatively simple step from locating the sea bottom to locating a shoal of fish.

初译⑧：因此，通过回声定位区分海底和鱼群相对比较简单。

学生评改：

评析：初译⑧在理解原文上出现了严重的失误。原文比较的对象是 locating the sea bottom 和 locating a shoal of fish 的技术，也就是从现有的测定海底的技术发展到测定鱼群的技术并不非常困难。但是，初译⑧错误地将比较对象理解为"海底"和"鱼群"，结果出现"区分海底和鱼群相对比较简单"的译文。出现这一严重失误的根源主要是句子结构和语法分析不当。在翻译过程中，如果遇到结构比较复杂的长难句时，译者的首要任务是厘清句子的主干和结构，这是正确理解原文的前提和关键。

改译：因此，技术上来讲，从探测海底发展到探测鱼群相对比较简单。

原文⑨：With experience and with improved apparatus, it is now possible not only to locate a shoal but to tell if it is herring, cod, or other well-known fish, by the pattern of its echo.

初译⑨：根据经验和改进了的仪器，现在不仅可以确定鱼群的位置，而且可以根据鱼群回声的模式辨别出是鲱鱼、鳕鱼，还是其他众所周知的鱼。

学生评改：_____

评析：初译⑨的主要问题在于表达方式不当。首先，"根据经验和改进了的仪器"读上去十分拗口，主要表现为搭配不当。在汉语中，"根据"可以和"经验"搭配，但是不能和"仪器"搭配。而且，"改进了的仪器"也是一种不地道的表达方式。鉴于此，可以考虑根据汉语的表达习惯，将其修改为"凭借经验和先进的仪器设备"或"随着经验的积累和仪器设备的不断改进"。其次，将 well-known fish 翻译为"众所周知的鱼"，从语体风格的角度来看并不恰当，建议将其修改为"人们熟知的鱼类"。

改译：随着经验的积累和仪器设备的不断改进，现在不仅可以定位鱼群，而且还可以通过回声波型判断其是鲱鱼、鳕鱼，还是其他人们熟知的鱼类。

Task B Translate the following text into Chinese.

The Standard Model of particle physics is one of the most powerful theories in science. It is, though, incomplete. It describes a suite of fundamental particles and the forces through which they interact, but it fails to include gravity and dark matter (mysterious stuff detectable at the moment only by its gravitational pull), and also cannot explain why there is more matter than antimatter in the universe.

CHAPTER 3 Physical Science

For these reasons, physicists have spent decades searching for ways to extend it, or at least for results that may provide a means of doing so. And on March 23rd, at a meeting called the Moriond Electroweak Physics Conference, a team from Europe's particle-physics laboratory, CERN, in Geneva, reported that they might have some.

The details are arcane. But they concern particles called beauty quarks which, themselves, form part of other particles called B-mesons. When beauty quarks decay, the daughter particles produced sometimes include a pair of what are known as charged leptons. These may be an electron and its antimatter equivalent, a positron, or two heavier leptons, a muon and an antimuon. The Standard Model predicts equal numbers of such pairs. But an analysis of results from the LHCB experiment, a purpose-built detector fitted to CERN's Large Hadron Collider (LHC), suggests electron-positron pairs are more abundant than muon pairs.

If confirmed, this could be the much sought crack into which researchers can insert a metaphorical crowbar to prise the Standard Model open and reveal what it is hiding—perhaps a fifth force of nature to go alongside gravity, electromagnetism, and the strong and weak nuclear forces.

Translation Tips 科技英语倍数的翻译方法

在科技英语中，倍数的增减是一种常见的表达方式。下文将针对科技英语中常见的倍数增减的翻译方法进行阐述。

 1. 倍数增加的译法

英语中常用的表示增加意义的动词包括 increase、grow、rise、multiply 等，表示倍数增加的常用句型有以下四种：

- 表示增加意义动词 + by + 倍数（N times），如 increase by N times；
- 表示增加意义动词 + to + 倍数（N times），如 grow to N times；
- 表示增加意义动词 + 倍数（N times），如 increase N times；
- 表示增加意义动词 + by + a factor of N，如 rise by a factor of N。

在英语中，倍数增加的表达都包括基数在内，因此上述四种句型表达的都是同一个意思，在汉译时可以表达为"增加到 N 倍"或"增加了（N-1）倍"。例如：

原文：The strength of the attraction **increases by four times** if the distance between the original charges is halved.

译文：如果原电荷之间的距离缩短一半，那么引力就会增加到原来的四倍。

本例中，原文中的倍数表达为 increases by four times，其意义就是"增加到原来的四倍"或"是原来的四倍"。部分学生一看到 by 就理解为"增加了"，结果错误地翻译为"增加到原来的五倍"。实际上，英语中所有关于倍数的表达句型都是将基数包括在内的，其意义都是一致的，即"是……的 N 倍"或"增加到 N 倍"。

 2. 倍数比较的译法

英语中常用的表示倍数比较的句型有以下三种：

- N times + 比较级 + than，如"A is N times larger than B."；
- 比较级 + than + by N times，如"A is larger than B by N times."；
- N times + as…as，如"A is N times as large as B."。

与倍数增加的翻译方法类似，倍数比较的表达也包括基数在内，因此一般翻译为"A 是 B 的 N 倍"或者"A 比 B 多（N-1）倍"。例如：

原文：In theory, compared to a conventional aircraft, the lift-to-drag ratio is better for the all-wing **by a factor of three**.

译文：理论上，全翼飞机的升阻比是常规飞机的三倍。

根据前述的翻译方法，本例中的 by a factor of three 可以直接翻译成"是常规飞机的三倍"，或者换算之后改为"比常规飞机提升两倍"。

 3. 倍数减少的译法

由于英汉两种语言表达习惯的不同，英语中涉及倍数减少的表达一般不翻译成"减少了 N 倍"，而应转换为分数，译为"是原来的 1/N"或"减少了 (N-1)/N"。

英语中常用的表示倍数减少的句型有以下五种：

- 表示减少意义动词 + by + 倍数（N times），如 decrease by N times；
- 表示减少意义动词 + 倍数（N times），如 decrease N times；
- 表示减少意义动词 + by + a factor of N，如 reduce by a factor of N；
- N times + 弱比较级 + than，如 N times smaller than；
- 表示减少意义动词 + N times + as…as，如 be shortened N times as long as。

与倍数增加和比较的译法相同，倍数减少的表达在汉译时只需将倍数转换为"是/为原来的 1/N"就可以。如果语言表达不通顺，则可以进行一定的转换。例如：

原文：Switching time of the new-type transistor is shortened **by three times**.
译文：新型晶体管的开关时间缩短为原来的 1/3（或缩短了 2/3）。

CHAPTER 4
Materials Science

Introduction

    Materials science has become more widely recognized as a specific and distinct field of science and engineering in recent years. Many of the most pressing scientific problems we currently face are due to the limitations of the materials that are available and, as a result, breakthroughs in materials science could have a significant impact on the future of technology. The interdisciplinary field of materials science involves the discovery and design of new materials, with an emphasis on solids. In this chapter, Text 1 is a passage for fast reading, introducing the popular nanotechnology; Text 2 is a passage for intensive reading on the magic material, graphene; and Text 3 is a passage for translation, discussing the development of LED. The learning objective of this chapter is to familiarize the learners with some grammatical features of EST at the sentence level and the translation techniques for negative sentences in EST.

Lead-in Questions

1. Why is nanotechnology so popular recently? Can you name some applications of nanotechnology in our life?

2. LED is an acronym for "light emitting diode", which is a device that produces light on electrical and electronic equipment. What advantages does LED have over traditional lights?

Section A Fast and Intensive Reading

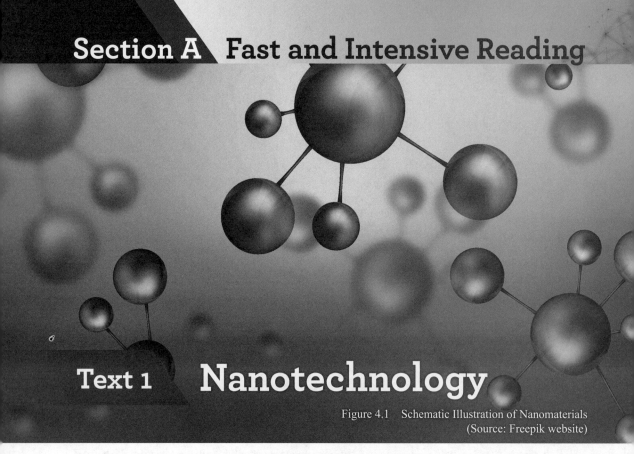

Text 1 Nanotechnology

Figure 4.1 Schematic Illustration of Nanomaterials
(Source: Freepik website)

A Nanotechnology deals with the understanding and control of matter at dimensions between approximately 1 and 100 nanometers, where unique phenomena enable novel applications. More specifically, nanotechnology is the imaging, modeling, measuring, design, characterization, production, and application of structures, devices, and systems by controlled manipulation of size and shape at the nanometer scale (atomic, molecular, and macromolecular scale) that produces structures, devices, and systems with at least one novel/superior characteristic or property.

B One of the problems facing this technology is the confusion about how to define nanotechnology. Most revolve around the study and control of phenomena and materials at length scales below 100 nm and quite often they make a comparison with a human hair, which is about 50,000 to 100,000 nm wide. For instance, in zero-dimensional (0D) nanomaterials, all the dimensions are measured within the nanoscale (no dimensions are larger than 100 nm); in two-dimensional nanomaterials (2D), two dimensions are outside the nanoscale; and in three-dimensional nanomaterials (3D) are materials that are not confined to the nanoscale in any dimension. This class can contain bulk powders, dispersions of nanoparticles, bundles of nanowires, and nanotubes as well as multi-nanolayers. Some definitions include a reference to molecular nanotechnology and "purists" argue that any definition needs to include a reference to "functional systems". The inaugural issue of *Nature Nanotechnology* asked 13 researchers from different areas what nanotechnology means to them and the responses, from enthusiastic to skeptical, reflect a variety of perspectives.

C   Another important criteria for the definition is the requirement that the nanostructure is man-made, i.e. a synthetically produced nanoparticle or nanomaterial. Otherwise, you would have to include every naturally formed biomolecule and material particle, in effect redefining much of chemistry and molecular biology as nanotech.

D   The term was coined in 1974 by Norio Taniguichi of Tokyo Science University to describe semiconductor processes such as thin-film deposition that deal with control on the order of nanometers. His definition still stands as the basic statement today: "Nanotechnology mainly consists of the processing of separation, consolidation, and deformation of materials by one atom or one molecule."

E   Unusual physical, chemical, and biological properties can emerge in materials at the nanoscale. These properties may differ in important ways from the properties of bulk materials and single atoms or molecules. The bulk properties of materials often change dramatically with nano-ingredients. Composites made from particles of nano-size ceramics or metals smaller than 100 nanometers can suddenly become much stronger than predicted by existing materials-science models. For example, metals with a so-called grain size of around 10 nanometers are as much as seven times harder and tougher than their ordinary counterparts with grain sizes in the hundreds of nanometers. The causes of these drastic changes stem from the weird world of quantum physics. The bulk properties of any material are merely the average of all the quantum forces affecting all the atoms. As you make things smaller and smaller, you eventually reach a point where the averaging no longer works.

F   The properties of materials can be different at the nanoscale for two main reasons:

- Surface Area: First, nanomaterials have a relatively larger surface area when compared to the same mass of materials produced in a larger form. This can make materials more chemically reactive (in some cases materials that are inert in their larger form are reactive when produced in their nanoscale form), and affect their strength or electrical properties.

- Quantum Size Effects: Second, quantum effects can begin to dominate the behavior of matter at the nanoscale—particularly at the lower end—affecting the optical, electrical, and magnetic behavior of materials. This effect describes the physics of electron properties in solids with great reductions in particle size. This effect does not come into play by going from macro to micro dimensions. However, it becomes dominant when the nanometer size range is reached.

G There are different ways of manipulating matter at the nanoscale. The two notions you hear most are top-down and bottom-up methods. Briefly, that means that you make a nanomaterial either by taking a block of material and removing the bits and pieces you don't want until you get the shape and size you do want (that's top-down), or you use nature's self-organizing processes (that's called self-assembly) to build something from the bottom-up. The key to using self-assembly as a controlled and directed fabrication process lies in designing the components that are required to self-assemble into desired patterns and functions.

H With regard to nanoscale materials, there are plenty of examples we could talk about here—nanoparticles, quantum dots, nanowires, nanofibers, ultrathin films, MXenes, etc. One example, though, that is exemplary of how an "old" material gets an exciting new life through nanoscale technologies is the element carbon. Natural carbon can exist in two very different types and is known to everyone: graphite and diamond. Three additional forms that were discovered between 1985 and 2004 have caused the current excitement among researchers about carbon nanomaterials—fullerenes.

I Current applications of nanomaterials include very thin coatings used, for example, in electronics and active surfaces (such as self-cleaning windows). In most applications, the nanomaterial will be fixed or embedded but in some, such as those used in cosmetics and in some environmental remediation applications, free nanoparticles are used. The ability to engineer materials to very high precision and accuracy (smaller than 100 nm) is leading to considerable benefits in a wide range of industrial sectors, for instance in the production of components for information and communication technology, automotive, and aerospace industries.

CHAPTER 4　Materials Science

J　Truly revolutionary nanotech products, materials, and applications, such as nanorobotics, are years in the future (some say only a few years; some say many years). What qualifies as "nanotechnology" today is basic research and development that is happening in laboratories all over the world. There are also numerous environmental, health, and safety issues associated with nanotechnology and nanomaterials. For instance, what happens if nanomaterials enter the body or the environment?

(Source: Nanowerk website)

Notes

fullerene: a molecule of carbon in the form of a hollow sphere, ellipsoid, tube, and many other shapes　富勒烯（一种完全由碳组成的中空分子，形状呈球形、椭球形、柱形或管状）

graphite: a soft black mineral that is a form of carbon, and is used to make pencils, lubricate machinery, and nuclear reactors　石墨

MXenes: In materials science, MXenes are a class of two-dimensional inorganic compounds (e.g., graphene, which is the most famous member of the two-dimensional materials family). These materials consist of a-few-atoms-thick layers of transition metal carbides or carbonitrides.　氮化物

nanorobotics: the emerging technology field creating machines or robots whose components are at or close to the scale of a nanometer　纳米机器人

quantum physics: Also known as quantum mechanics or quantum theory, including quantum field theory (量子场论), it is a fundamental branch of physics concerned with processes involving, for example, atoms and photons. 量子物理

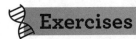

Exercises

Task A Identify the paragraph from which each of the following statements is derived. You may choose a paragraph more than once. Each paragraph in the above text is marked with a letter.

1. Nanotechnology has great significance because at the nanoscale some super physical, chemical, and biological properties can occur.

2. It is not an easy thing to give nanotechnology a proper definition.

3. The fascination with nanotechnology stems from the unique quantum effects and larger surface area at the nanoscale.

4. Nanostructure is synthetic which excludes all natural molecules and particles.

5. There are mainly two methods to change matter at the nanoscale.

6. Dimensions between approximately 1 and 100 nanometers are known as the nanoscale.

7. Nanotechnology can also be used in the making of parts for information and communication technology.

8. One of the natural forms of carbon is called as graphite.

9. The real revolutionary nanotechnology is yet to happen and we need to be precautious about the development.

10. The person who named nanotechnology is a Japanese and his definition is still considered as the basis today.

Task B Work in groups to discuss the following topic and share your opinions with the class.

How to Balance Benefits and Responsibilities?

The emergence of nanotechnology has led to several ethical concerns associated with the possibility of health and environmental hazards, including the potential toxicity of nanoparticles and their effects on human health and the environment, in addition to the broader implications for society. How can we strike a balance between maximizing the benefits of this technology and ensuring that it is utilized in an accountable and sustainable way?

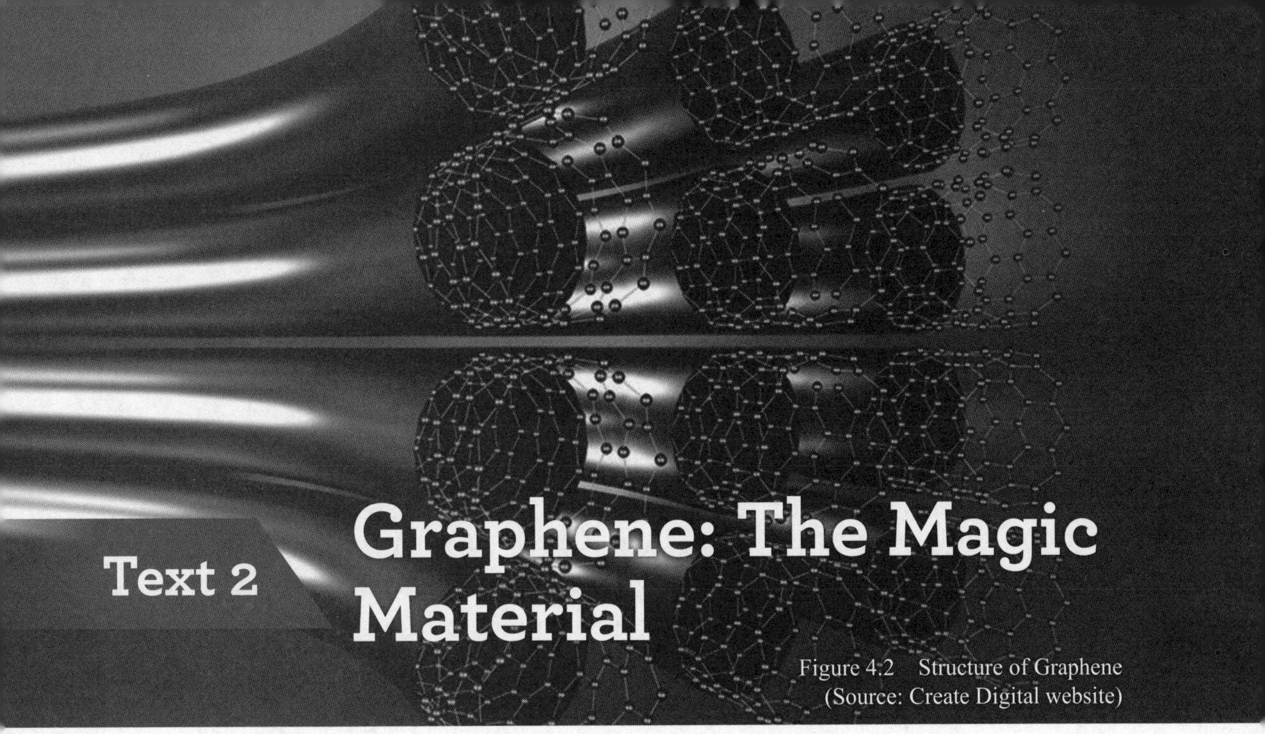

Text 2

Graphene: The Magic Material

Figure 4.2 Structure of Graphene
(Source: Create Digital website)

Throughout history, the progress of human civilization has largely relied on its capability to discover, extract, and utilize different materials from Earth. Each new material provided benefits that not only equipped the early civilizations for survival but also enabled them to defeat enemies and build a better life. Back in the Stone Age, humans used stone tools. This era later developed into the Bronze Age where, for the first time, humans began working with metal. This further progressed into the Iron Age during which people manufactured tools from iron and steel. Every subsequent age is known for its newly discovered materials that brought new technologies and further development to society.

The age we are living in, in the twenty-first century can be recognized as the Carbon Age. Carbon is the basic element of life, but it may soon become the basic element of the rest of the world as well. Graphite, the stable thermodynamic state of carbon under environmental conditions, has been studied and used by humankind for centuries. When you draw a line on the paper and put pressure on it, then the color turns dark. This happens because graphite consists of thousands of identical layers piled on top of each other; the more layers you leave on paper, the darker the color is. A single layer of graphite is called **graphene** and has a thickness of a billionth of a meter.

graphene 石墨烯

The discovery and synthesis of graphene is one of the most remarkable advances in materials over the last decades. It is the building block of many carbon allotropes (different physical forms in which elements can exist). Graphene has a perfect **hexagonal arrangement** of carbon atoms held together by covalent bonds into a honeycomb sheet. According to Dr. Savjani, graphene is the easiest to imagine as a honeycomb sheet of carbon atoms that is completely flat.

hexagonal arrangement 六边形排列

A Canadian theoretical physicist, Phillip Wallace, initially conceptualized graphene in 1947. He predicted that if a coated sheet of graphite were to be isolated, it would have certain abnormal and interesting qualities. It was practically discovered by Andre Geim and Konstantin Novoselov at the University of Manchester during their Friday evening experiment in 2004 by using a technique called "Sticky Tape". They used an adhesive tape to extract the graphene layers from graphite and placed them on silicon wafers. They were awarded the Nobel Prize for this simple yet groundbreaking experiment in 2010 which opened the doors to more research.

Graphene has unique characteristics as it retains its original size and shape even if you bend and twist it. Two-dimensional sheets of atoms, also called monolayers, can be made of other materials like boron, silicon, germanium, and phosphorus; they have the suffix *-ene* tacked in their names (like germanene and **phosphorene**). Like graphene, they also have some unique properties. Phosphorene has some interesting electrical properties due to the ability of phosphorus to form five bonds (carbon, on the other hand, can only form four bonds).

phosphorene 磷烯

CHAPTER 4 Materials Science

There are many materials competing with each other for the benefits they provide but graphene is one of the rising stars with many benefits.

Graphene has a tensile strength of 130 **gigapascals**—100 times stronger than steel of the same thickness. Therefore, whenever we think of space elevators, graphene will play a significant role because of its strength. The storage density of **lithium-ion batteries** is increased about two to three times by the addition of graphene to it. There is no bandgap (energy difference between the valence band and conduction band) found in graphene. If graphene is not having any bandgap, then its electrons can occupy any energy level. This creates interesting opportunities in manufacturing solar cells. However, it is not always desirable to have no band gaps. For instance, a bandgap is needed for switching devices like transistors. An impurity added to the graphene can help to accomplish this too.

One of the astonishing characteristics of graphene is it's extremely lightweight, due to which it can be used to make large buildings and bridges. Graphene is transparent due to its ability to absorb 2.3% of the light that shines on it. Moreover, graphene has high **electron mobility**, a measure of how easily electrons travel in a substance, which is 100 times that of silicon. Boosting the movement of electrons is a way to reduce the size of devices and make them work faster. Thus, graphene is the strongest material in the world, stronger than steel but lighter than aluminum and harder than a diamond but more flexible than rubber.

Graphene can transform three major areas: computing and electronics, energy storage, and structural engineering. Ultra-fast graphene computers will not only make all our personal devices much faster but will also open many new areas, particularly in implanted medical electronics.

gigapascal 吉帕斯卡（物理单位）

lithium-ion battery 锂离子电池

electron mobility 电子迁移

Carbon nanotube (rolled-up sheets of graphene) is one of the most well-known applications in the field of structural engineering. It will create new opportunities, not only due to its low weight and high tensile strength but also because of its ability to make materials that are electrically and thermally non-conductive.

Graphene offers numerous future applications. For instance, it can be used for making flexible displays because of its unique property of folding and bending. Moreover, derivatives of graphene (graphene oxides) can be used for drug delivery, as nano drugs bound to graphene oxide sheets can be used to deliver drugs for anticancer therapies without causing any **toxicity**. If methods for graphene's production and processing can be developed and exploited on an industrial scale, this will create a technology boom not only in physical and electrical engineering but also in bioengineering. Some production issues or costs may render some of the above uses impracticable, but if even a fraction of this magic material's potential can be realized, it will revolutionize the world we live in.

toxicity 毒性

(Source: Britannica website)

Exercises

Task A **Decide whether the following statements are true (T) or false (F).**

1. Graphene is a completely flat honeycomb sheet of carbon atoms that has a thickness of a millionth of a meter.
2. Graphene was practically discovered by a Canadian theoretical physicist, Phillip Wallace, in 1947.
3. Graphene is the strongest material in the world as it has a tensile strength of 130 gigapascals.
4. Graphene can be used to make large buildings and bridges because it is extremely lightweight.

CHAPTER 4 Materials Science

5. Nowadays, graphene is widely used in computing and electronics, energy storage, and structural engineering.

Task B Choose the word or phrase which is closest in meaning to the underlined part in each sentence.

1. Throughout history, the progress of human civilization has largely relied on its capability to discover, extract, and utilize different materials from Earth.
   A. build   B. dig   C. develop   D. use

2. The discovery and synthesis of graphene is one of the most remarkable advances in materials over the last decades.
   A. production   B. application   C. noticing   D. spreading

3. Graphene has unique characteristics as it retains its original size and shape even if you bend and twist it.
   A. constructs   B. changes   C. keeps   D. contains

4. Phosphorene has some interesting electrical properties due to the ability of phosphorus to form five bonds (carbon, on the other hand, can only form four bands).
   A. possessions   B. characteristics   C. forms   D. connections

5. If methods for graphene's production and processing can be developed and exploited on an industrial scale, this will create a technology boom not only in physical and electrical engineering but also in bioengineering.
   A. enhanced   B. used   C. performed   D. treated

Task C Answer the following questions based on the text.

1. What is graphene?

2. Why does the color turn dark when you draw a line on the paper and put pressure on it?

3. Why were Andre Geim and Konstantin Novoselov awarded the Noble Prize?

4. What properties make graphene one of the rising stars among competitive materials?

5. What benefits can graphene bring to common people's daily life?

Reading Tips 科技英语的句法特点（一）

科技英语在句子层面的特点非常鲜明和突出，熟悉并掌握科技英语的句法特点可以显著提高科技语篇的阅读效率和理解准确度。

1. 呈现名词化倾向

名词化（nominalization）是指为了满足表达和修辞的需要，动词、形容词和副词转化成名词或名词词组的语言现象。科技英语中的名词化现象十分普遍，是科技语篇句法结构的主要特点之一。首先，科技语篇需要客观叙述，尽力排除主观成分，而名词化结构的使用可以省略人称代词，更适宜阐明原理、定义等客观过程描述，使行文严谨、客观。其次，名词表达的含义从本质上看更为肯定和稳定，而动词表达的状态短暂易变，这在一定程度上会影响内容的可信度和稳定性。最后，名词化结构的使用还可以避免出现冗长繁复的句子，达到言简意赅的效果。试着对比以下句子的表达效果：

- **Original:** The moving parts of a machine are often oiled so that friction may be greatly reduced.

  Revised: The moving parts of a machine are often oiled for **a great reduction of** friction.

- **Original:** Energy can neither be created nor destroyed, although its form can be changed.

  Revised: Energy can neither be created nor destroyed in spite of **its changing form**.

- **Original:** You can rectify this fault if you insert a wedge.

  Revised: Rectification of this fault is achieved by **the insertion of** a wedge.

需要注意的是，有些英语动作性名词变复数以后，会从不可数名词变为可数名词，同时词义也有较大变化，在阅读理解时应注意这一细节带来的词义转变。例如，organization 指"较抽象、笼统的组织和筹备工作"，而 organizations 则指具体的一些组织、团体或机构；inclusion 指"包括""包含"，而 inclusions 指被包含的人或物；observation 指"观察和监测的动作或行为"，而 observations 指观察到的具体情况和结果等。

2. 大量使用非谓语动词

非谓语动词（non-finite verb）是指在句中充当除谓语以外的句子成分的动词形式。

动词的非谓语形式包括不定式、动名词和分词（现在分词和过去分词）。在科技英语中，使用非谓语动词既可以对修饰的成分进行限定和说明，还可以大大简化句子结构，避免复杂的主从复合结构，使句子既不累赘拖沓又精练准确。例如：

- It is very difficult **to measure the passing current in insulators**.（不定式做主语）
- The parts **to be jointed** are usually heated to a certain temperature.（不定式做定语）
- **Paying for products with a fingerprint**, rather than checks, cards, or electronic devices, is among the newest cashless options at the checkout.（动名词做主语）
- Once common functions are written in assembly language, they could then be copied into a new program without **having to be written again**.（动名词做宾语）
- Particles **bearing like charges** tend to repel one another, whereas particles **bearing unlike charges** tend to attract one another.（现在分词做定语）
- In a solid or liquid, the molecules are much closer together, **resulting in much more material in a given volume**.（现在分词做状语）
- While **held at rest at a certain height**, no mechanical work being done, the object definitely obtains the ability to do something.（过去分词做状语）

3. 广泛使用逻辑连接词

逻辑连接词是指在语篇中起着重要连接作用的词汇和短语。它们是实现语篇连贯的主要方式，能反映语篇前后的语义关系。通过连接词的运用，人们可以了解句子之间的语义关系，甚至可以经前句从逻辑上预见后句的语义。科技英语中广泛使用逻辑连接词，常见的类型如下：

- 表示列举：first; take...for example; except; to illustrate; be considered a classical example of...
- 表示强调：indeed; in particular; in reality; after all; above all; significantly; interestingly; in fact; as a matter of fact; especially; obviously; clearly; actually; surely; apparently...
- 表示比较：similarly; likewise; like; in the same manner; equally; compared with; in comparison with...
- 表示对比：but; by contrast; in contrast with; although; even though; while; whilst; whereas; on the other hand; on the contrary; unlike; instead; conversely;

different from; however; nevertheless; otherwise; despite...
- 表示递进：in addition; moreover; besides...
- 表示因果：for this reason; due to; thanks to; as; since; owing to; therefore; accordingly; the reason for...lies in; in virtue of; in consequence of; on the ground of; consequently; as a consequence...
- 表示转移话题：now; incidentally; by the way; to change the subject...
- 表示总结：on the whole; to sum up; in brief; in summary; to put it simply; to conclude; to summarize...
- 表示让步：after all; in spite of; despite; admittedly...

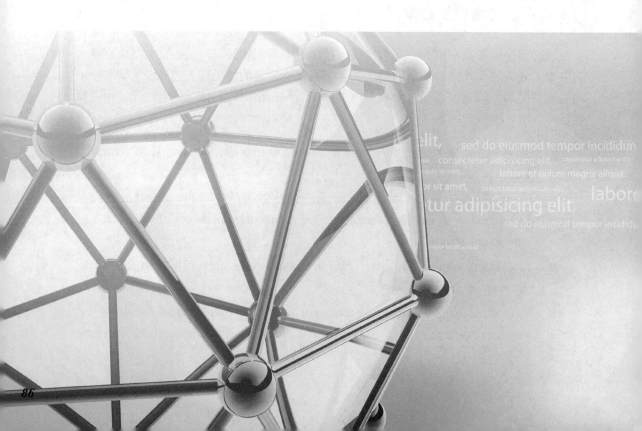

Section B Translation

Text 3 — Small Lights with Big Potential

Figure 4.3   LED Lamp
(Source: Freepik website)

LED is a semiconductor light source that emits light when current flows through it. Electrons in the semiconductor recombine with electron holes, releasing energy in the form of photons.

Currently, the LED lamp is popular due to its efficiency and many believe it is a "new" technology. The LED as we know it has been around for over 50 years. The recent development of white LEDs is what has brought it into the public eye as a replacement for other white light sources.

LEDs have the following advantages:

- Energy efficient source of light for short distances and small areas. The typical LED requires only 30–60 milliwatts to operate.
- Durable and shockproof unlike glass bulb lamp types.
- Directional nature is useful for some applications like reducing stray light pollution on streetlights.

As for disadvantages, they are as follows:

- May be unreliable in outside applications with great variations in summer/winter temperatures. More work is being done now to solve this problem.
- Semiconductors are sensitive to being damaged by heat, so large heat

sinks must be employed to keep powerful arrays cool; sometimes a fan is required. This adds to cost and a fan greatly reduces the energy efficient advantage of LEDs. It is also prone to failure which leads to unit failure.

- Circuit board solder and thin copper connections crack when flexed and cause sections of arrays to go out.

- Rare earth metals used in LEDs are subject to price control monopolies by certain nations.

- Reduced lumen output over time.

① LEDs create light by electroluminescence in a semiconductor material. ② Electroluminescence is the phenomenon of a material emitting light when electric current or an electric field is passed through it—this happens when electrons are sent through the material and fill electron holes. ③ An electron hole exists where an atom lacks electrons (negatively charged) and therefore has a positive charge. ④ Semiconductor materials like germanium or silicon can be "doped" to create and control the number of electron holes.

⑤ Doping is the adding of other elements to the semiconductor material to change its properties. ⑥ By doping a semiconductor you can make two separate types of semiconductors in the same crystal. ⑦ The boundary between the two types is called a p-n junction. ⑧ The junction only allows current to pass through it one way; this is why they are used as diodes.

LEDs are made using p-n junctions. As electrons pass through one crystal to the other, they fill electron holes. They emit photons (light). This is also how the semiconductor laser works.

Phosphors are used to help filter the light output of the LED. They create a more pure "harsh" color. Engineers had to figure out how to control the angle at which the light escapes the semiconductor; this "light cone" is very narrow. They figured out how to make light refract or bounce off all surfaces of the semiconductor crystal to intensify the light output. This is why LED displays traditionally have been best viewed from one angle.

(Source: The Edison Tech Center website)

CHAPTER 4　Materials Science

Exercises

Task A **Review the original translation of the underlined sentences in the source text and make any necessary revisions. Then learn how to improve your revisions from the analysis and modification of the translation provided.**

这篇短文的主题是发光二极管（LED），主要介绍了它的优势、不足及发光原理等。文中画线部分针对发光原理展开，译文评价如下：

原文①：LEDs create light by electroluminescence in a semiconductor material.

初译①：发光二极管通过半导体材料中的电致发光来发光。

学生评改：_____

评析：原文①介绍了发光二极管的发光原理，即电致发光。初译将 by electroluminescence 处理为"通过……电致发光"的方法不够准确，因为读者读完之后并不清楚电致发光究竟是某种物质还是某种原理。因此，翻译时应采取增译的方法将其补充完整，译为"电致发光原理"或"电致发光现象"。需要注意的是，"通过……原理"这种搭配并不合理，可以考虑修改为"利用电致发光原理"。如此一来，译文就比较明确和通顺了。

改译：发光二极管（LED）利用半导体材料中的电致发光原理来产生光。

原文②：Electroluminescence is the phenomenon of a material emitting light when electric current or an electric field is passed through it—this happens when electrons are sent through the material and fill electron holes.

初译②：电致发光是一种材料在有电流或电场通过时发光的现象，这种现象发生在电子通过材料并填充电子空穴时。

学生评改：_____

> **评析**：本句承接上一句，进一步界定什么是电致发光。原文②由两个小句构成，第二个小句对这种现象做进一步解释。初译②的前半句存在语序不当的问题，因为译文完全按照原文的顺序翻译，并不符合汉语的表达习惯。原文中 passed through it 中的 it 指代的是"材料"，所以可以将"材料"放在"电流或电场"之后做宾语。后半句也存在同样的问题。英语原文是一个主从复合句，主句在前，状语从句在后，而汉语则习惯将状语从句前置，之后再说主句，即"当电子通过材料并填充电子空穴时，这种现象就会发生"。
>
> **改译**：电致发光是指当电流或电场通过材料时发光的现象——当电子通过材料并填充电子空穴时，这种现象就会发生。

> **原文③**：An electron hole exists where an atom lacks electrons (negatively charged) and therefore has a positive charge.
>
> **初译③**：电子空穴存在于原子缺少电子（带负电）的地方，因此具有正电荷。

学生评改：_____

> **评析**：原文③是一个含有因果关系的并列句，其中前一小句包含一个 where 引导的定语从句。初译采取直译法，将定语从句处理为前置定语，这是一种常见的译法，但是译为"原子缺少电子（带负电）的地方"并不可取。定语从句的翻译方法有多种，其中将定语从句转换为状语从句是一种非常有效的方法。此处，通过分析可以发现原文中两个小句之间存在因果关系，即"电子空穴是由于原子缺少电子而形成的"。因此，翻译时可以将定语从句转换为原因状语从句。另外，初译把 and 引导的小句翻译为"因此具有正电荷"与前文的"带负电"不对应，建议修改为"因此带正电"。
>
> **改译**：电子空穴是由于原子缺少（带负电的）电子而形成的，因此带正电。

CHAPTER 4　Materials Science

原文④：Semiconductor materials like germanium or silicon can be "doped" to create and control the number of electron holes.

初译④：像锗或硅这样的半导体材料可以被"掺杂"以产生和控制电子空穴的数量。

学生评改：_____

评析：从单句翻译的角度来看，初译④尚可以接受；但如果从语篇的角度来看，则显得十分突兀，缺乏连贯性。因为前文没有提及任何半导体材料，此处在句首突然列举"像锗或硅这样的半导体材料"就显得思维跳跃幅度过大、文本可接受性差。此外，根据原文可以看出，锗或硅只是作者列举半导体材料的两个代表，实际上其他半导体材料也具有上述特性。而"像锗或硅这样的半导体材料"这样的表述会让读者误以为这种特性仅限于这两种材料。鉴于此，修改后的译文将半导体材料做主语，列举的两种材料则放在括号内，这样处理既可以明确主语为"一些半导体材料"，又避免了前后文逻辑不连贯的问题。

改译：一些半导体材料（如锗或硅）可以通过"掺杂"的方式来产生和控制电子空穴的数量。

原文⑤⑥：Doping is the adding of other elements to the semiconductor material to change its properties. By doping a semiconductor you can make two separate types of semiconductors in the same crystal.

初译⑤⑥：掺杂是在半导体材料中添加其他元素以改变其性能。通过对半导体的掺杂，你可以在同一晶体中制造两种不同类型的半导体。

学生评改：_____

评析：原文⑤和⑥介绍了半导体材料的掺杂特性。总体来看，初译⑤基本没有问题，而初译⑥的表述欠佳，主要体现在 you can make two separate types of semiconductors in the same crystal 的翻译上。一方面，在科技语篇翻译中，为了体现客观性，一般尽量避免使用人称主语，此处可以将人称代词 you 进行省略，这并不影响译文的通顺性。另一方面，"在同一晶体中制造两种不同类型的半导体"这种说法不够明确，令读者比较费解。通过查询专业知识可知，同一块晶体两侧通过掺杂不同的杂质可以形成 p 型半导体和 n 型半导体。也就是说，通过掺杂，一块晶体可以被制成两种不同类型半导体的复合体。基于此，可以将初译修改为"可以将同一种晶体制成两种不同类型半导体的复合体"。

改译：掺杂是指在半导体材料中添加其他元素以改变其性能。通过对半导体材料进行掺杂，可以将同一种晶体制成两种不同类型半导体的复合体。

原文⑦⑧：The boundary between the two types is called a p-n junction. The junction only allows current to pass through it one way; this is why they are used as diodes.

初译⑦⑧：这两种类型之间的边界称为 p-n 结。p-n 结只允许电流单向通过，这就是为什么它们被作为二极管来使用。

学生评改：_____

_____

_____

评析：原文⑦和⑧的联系比较紧密，可以放在一起讨论。其中，初译⑦的第一个问题在于 two types 的翻译"两种类型"的语义不明确，需要增译为"两种类型半导体"。第二个问题在于 boundary 译为"边界"并不准确，因为"边界"是指位置，而 p-n 结是物质，二者搭配不当。尽管 boundary 在词典中的释义为"边界"或"界限"，但是此处需要结合语境进行具体化引申，可以考虑翻译为"接合部"。而初译⑧中"这就是为什么它们被作为二极管来使用"的表述过于口语化，建议修改为"这就是它们用作发光二极管的原因"。

CHAPTER 4 **Materials Science**

> 改译：这两种类型半导体之间的接合部称为p-n结。p-n结只允许电流单向通过，这就是它们用作发光二极管的原因。

Task B Translate the following text into Chinese.

Scientists have found a new way to structure carbon at the nanoscale, making a material that is superior to diamond on the strength-to-density ratio. While the tiny carbon lattice has been fabricated and tested in the lab, it is a very long way off practical use. But this new approach could help us build stronger and lighter materials in the future—which is something that is of great interest to industries such as aerospace and aviation. What we are talking about here is something known as a nanolattices-porous structure like the one in the image above that is made up of three-dimensional carbon struts and braces. Due to their unique structure, they are incredibly strong and lightweight. Usually, these nanolattices are based around a cylindrical framework (they are called beam-nanolattices). But the team has now created plate-nanolattices structures based around tiny plates.

This subtle shift may not sound like much, but the researchers say it can make a big difference when it comes to strength. Based on early experiments and calculations, the plate approach promises a 639% increase in strength and a 522% increase in rigidity over the beam-nanolattice approach.

Translation Tips 否定句的翻译方法

英语中的否定形式灵活多样，否定句式种类繁多，加之英汉两种语言在表达否定概念的词汇、语法、句型方面存在诸多差异，因此英语否定句的翻译是科技语篇理解和学习中的重要内容。英语中的常见否定句型包括完全否定、部分否定、双重否定，特殊否定表达包括意义否定句、否定的延续、否定的转移等。其中，特殊否定表达的翻译难度较大，下文将重点探讨。

1. 意义否定句

意义否定句是指某些句子的语法结构是肯定形式，但其内容却表达了否定的意义。这类句型中通常包含有否定意义的单词或词组，如 lack、wonder、fail、impossible、far from、in the absence of 等。在翻译意义否定句时，译者需要以恰当的方式将其否定意义翻译出来。例如：

原文：The performance of the machine **is short of** the requirements.
译文：这台机器的性能没有达到要求。（be short of 短语含有否定意义）
原文：The angularity of the parts is **too great for** proper assembly.
译文：零件斜度太大，不易装配。（too...for 短语含有否定意义）

2. 否定的转移

否定的转移是指否定形式在某个句子成分中，而否定的信息焦点却在其他句子成分中；或者否定形式在主句，但否定的信息焦点却在从句。这是由英语的表达习惯和思维方式决定的，汉译时译者需要根据否定的信息焦点进行否定转移。

（1）句子成分的否定转移

句子成分的否定转移是指英语中否定的是宾语，但汉译时否定的是谓语；或者英语中否定的是状语，但汉译时否定的是谓语等情况。例如：

原文：We know of no effective way to store the Sun's heat.
译文：我们不知道储藏太阳热量的有效方法。（否定宾语转为否定谓语）
原文：On no conditions should the circuit be overloaded.
译文：电路在任何情况下都不得超负荷。（否定状语转为否定谓语）

（2）主句从句的否定转移

在某些情况下，从形式上看，英语中否定的是主句，但从意义上看，否定的却是从句，此时汉译时译者需要对从句进行否定。例如：

原文：The object did not move because it was pushed.
译文：该物体并非由于受到推力作用而移动。（主句否定转移为从句否定）
原文：They don't think the inactive gas could support combustion.
译文：他们认为惰性气体无法助燃。（主句否定转移为从句否定）

3. 否定的延续

在科技英语中，译者经常会遇到这种情况：两个谓语并列，前一个谓语有否定词，而后一个谓语没有否定词。在这种情况下，否定是否延续（后一个谓语动词是否需要否定）取决于谓语动词之前是否有情态动词或助动词。

如果前一个谓语动词带有情态动词或助动词，后一个谓语没有情态动词或助动词，那么否定延续。例如：

原文：The traditional technique can't be used to locate the sea bottom or locate a shoal of fish.
译文：传统方法既不能测定海底的位置，也无法定位鱼群。

如果前后两个谓语动词都带有情态动词或助动词，那么否定不延续。例如：

原文：Thus, when coal is piled too deeply, heat formed by slow oxidation of coal within the pile can't find a way out and may cause the pile to catch fire itself.
译文：因此，当煤堆得太厚，煤在煤堆里缓慢氧化产生的热量无法散出，就有可能引起煤堆自燃。

CHAPTER 5
Biomedical Science

Introduction

Biomedical science is the application of the principles of natural sciences to medicine, which is devoted to understanding the human body and our ability to control it during health and disease. The discipline of biomedical science combines the fields of biology and medicine to focus on the health of both humans and animals. Biomedical scientists develop new treatments and therapies for illnesses, diseases, and disabilities. They research medical conditions such as cancer, diabetes, anemia, stress, and aging. In this chapter, Text 1 is a passage for fast reading, talking about the discovery of artemisinin; Text 2 is a passage for intensive reading, introducing heat shock proteins; and Text 3 is a passage for translation, reporting the genetic sequencing of Ebola. The learning objective of this chapter is to familiarize the learners with other grammatical features of EST at the sentence level and the translation techniques for adverbial clauses in EST.

Lead-in Questions

1. Why do people believe that biomedical scientists are at the heart of multi-disciplinary teams in healthcare?

2. What is the significance of DNA sequencing? Why is it called the gold standard for microorganism identification?

Section A Fast and Intensive Reading

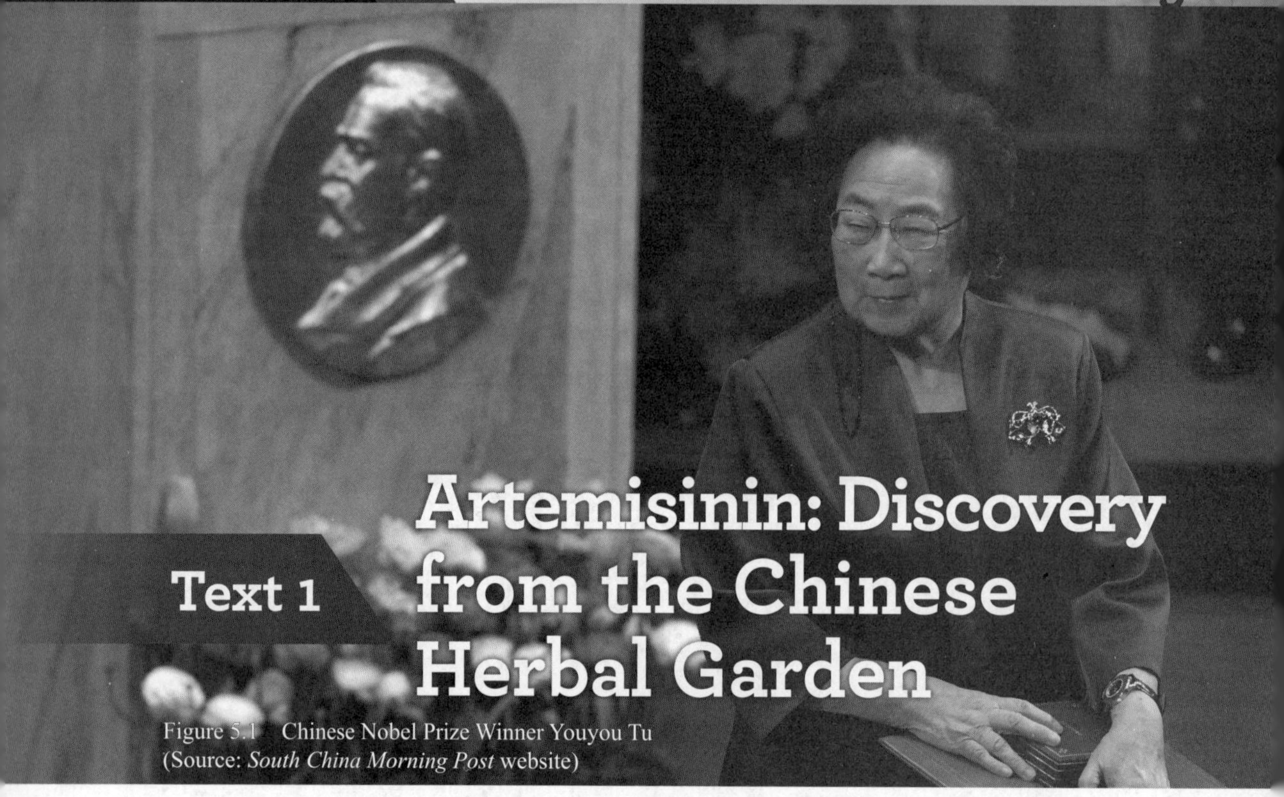

Text 1   Artemisinin: Discovery from the Chinese Herbal Garden

Figure 5.1   Chinese Nobel Prize Winner Youyou Tu
(Source: *South China Morning Post* website)

A   This year's Lasker DeBakey Clinical Research Award goes to Youyou Tu for the discovery of artemisinin and its use in the treatment of malaria—a medical advance that has saved millions of lives across the globe, especially in the developing world.

B   The future benefits of many seminal discoveries in basic biomedical sciences are not always obvious in the short run. But for a handful of others, the impact on human health is immediately clear. Such is the case for the discovery by Youyou Tu and her colleagues of artemisinin (also known as Qinghaosu) for the treatment of malaria. Artemisinin has been the frontline treatment since the late 1990s and has saved countless lives, especially among the world's poorest children.

C   Malaria is a life-threatening epidemic disease. It was, however, effectively treated and controlled by chloroquine and quinoline for a long period of time until the development of drug-resistant malaria plasmodium parasites, namely plasmodium falciparum, in the late 1960s following the catastrophic failure of a global attempt to eradicate malaria. Resurgence of malaria and rapidly increased mortality posed a significant global challenge, especially in the Southeast Asian countries. In the 1960s, the Division of Experimental Therapeutics at the

CHAPTER 5 Biomedical Science

Walter Reed Army Institute of Research (WRAIR) in Washington, D.C. launched programs to search for novel therapies to support the U.S. military presence in Southeast Asia. U.S. military force involved in the Vietnam War suffered massive casualties due to disability caused by malaria infection.

D   The long journey searching for antimalarial drugs for Youyou Tu and her colleagues began with a collection of relevant information and recipes from traditional Chinese medicine. Malaria was one of the epidemic diseases with the most comprehensive records in traditional Chinese medical literature, such as *Zhou Li* (《周礼》), a classical book in ancient China published in the Zhou Dynasty (1046–256 B.C.). Other literature includes the *Inner Canon of the Yellow Emperor* (《黄帝内经》) published around the time of the Chun Qiu and Qin Dynasties (770–207 B.C.), the *Synopsis of Prescriptions of the Golden Chamber* (《金匮要略》) published in the Han Dynasty (206 B.C.–220 A.D.), the *General Treatise on the Causes and Symptoms of Diseases* (《诸病源候论》) published in the Sui Dynasty (581–618 A.D.), the *Qian Jin Fang* or *Prescriptions Worth a Thousand Pieces of Gold* (《千金方》) and the *Wai Tai Mi Yao* or *Secret Medical Essentials of a Provincial Governor* (《外台密要》) published in the Tang Dynasty (618–907 A.D.), *A Book on Malaria* (《痎疟论疏》) published in the Ming Dynasty (1368–1644 A.D.) and the *Malignant Malaria Guide* (《瘴疟指南》) published in the Qing Dynasty (1644–1911 A.D.), the *Prescription for Universal Relief* (《普济方》) published in the Ming Dynasty (1368–1644 A.D.), etc.

E   During their search, Youyou Tu and her colleagues investigated more than 2,000 recipes of Chinese traditional herbs, compiling 640 recipes that might have some antimalarial activity. They tested in a rodent malaria model more than 200 recipes with Chinese traditional herbs and 380 extracts from the herbs. Among the promising results, extracts from Artemisia annua L. (Qinghao), a type of wormwood native to Asia, were shown to inhibit parasite growth by 68%. Follow-up studies, however, only achieved 12% to 40% inhibition. Professor Tu reasoned that the low inhibition could be due to a low concentration of the active ingredient in the preparation and began to improve the methods of extraction. After reading the ancient Chinese medical description, "take one bunch of Qinghao, soak in two sheng (~0.4 liters) of water, wring it out to obtain the juice, and ingest it in its entirety" in *The Handbook of Prescriptions for Emergency Treatments* (《肘后备急方》) by Ge Hong (283–363 A.D.) during the Jin Dynasty (265–420 A.D.), she realized that traditional methods of boiling and high-temperature extraction could damage the active ingredient. Indeed, a much better extract was obtained after switching from ethanol to ether extraction at a lower temperature.

F   However, the extract was still toxic. Professor Tu then further removed from the extract an acidic portion that contained no antimalarial activity, leaving a neutral extract with reduced toxicity and improved antimalarial activity. The neutral extract, termed extract number 191, was tested in the mouse malaria, Plasmodium berghei, and achieved 100% inhibition in October 1971. She presented her findings at a 523 meeting held in Nanjing on March 8, 1972, providing some critical parameters for other teams to quickly obtain pure artemisinin crystals. Although Tu's team struggled to obtain high-quality crystals from the plant in the following months, two teams (Zeyuan Luo, Yunnan Institute of Drug Research and the late Zhangxing Wei, Shandong Institute of Traditional Chinese Medicine), using the information and methods she used, soon obtained pure crystals from Artemisia. annua L. that were highly active against rodent malaria parasites. Tests in humans by Guoqiao Li, Guangzhou University of Chinese Medicine, using the artemisinin crystals from Yunnan Institute of Drug Research, showed good activity against malaria infection.

G   Interestingly, the paper describing artemisinin's X-ray crystal structure, pharmacology, and efficacy against non-severe and severe cerebral malaria listed no specific authors, who were identified instead as the Qinghaosu Antimalarial Coordinating Research Group (1979). The paper showed that artemisinin is a sesquiterpene lactone with an endoperoxide, and that the endoperoxide is required for its antimalarial activity. In 1985, Klayman, working in the U.S. at the WRAIR, described the isolation of the same compound and its structure from Artemisia annua L. (sweet wormwood), which grew along the shores of the Potomac River. Klayman pointed out that there are few naturally occurring endoperoxides described in plants. Although numerous hydroperoxides had been tested at the WRAIR, none were found to have antimalarial activity.

H   Two clinical studies headed by Professor Gouqiao Li compared artemisinin and mefloquine. These studies were the first to suggest that combination therapy should be considered to prevent the recurrence and development of resistance (Jiang et al., 1982; Li et al., 1984). Artemisinin works quickly within hours compared to mefloquine's slow parasite clearance, but because of its short half-life, artemisinin requires another drug in combination to obtain a cure. Patients recovered so quickly after taking artemisinin that they would not continue treatment after they felt better and thus were ultimately not cured. Such incomplete treatment may promote drug resistance. Li's group also developed suppositories containing artemisinin to treat cerebral malaria that are now being used in field clinics in Africa. Shortening the time to treatment by the use of suppositories improves survival.

I　After learning this important discovery by the Chinese, Nick White, who was working in Thailand as a professor at Oxford, began the study of artemisinin derivatives. He confirmed its rapid activity and the need for a partner drug to clear the parasitemia and became the primary proponent for the use of artemisinin derivatives in combination therapy, which is now the standard treatment worldwide. In 2010, he was honored by the Canadian Gairdner Award for this important work.

J　Project 523 developed, in addition to artemisinin, a number of products that are used in combination with artemisinin, including lumefantrine, piperaquine, and pyronaridine. Their success reflects the unique spirit of collaboration from a large number of scientists and institutions involved in the search for antimalarial drugs.

(Source: National Center for Biotechnology Information website)

Notes

artemisinin: Also known as Qinghaosu, its semi-synthetic derivatives are a group of drugs that possess the most rapid action of all current drugs against Plasmodium falciparum malaria.　青蒿素

ethanol: the type of alcohol in alcoholic drinks, also used as a fuel or solvent 乙醇；酒精

malaria: a disease that causes fever and shivering (shaking of the body) caused by the bite of some types of mosquitoes　疟疾

Plasmodium: Commonly known as the malaria parasite, it is a large genus of parasitic protozoa.　疟原虫（一类单细胞、寄生性的原生动物）

wormwood: a plant with a bitter flavor, used in making alcoholic drinks and medicines　蒿；洋艾（有些具苦味，可入药或用来制苦艾酒等）

Exercises

Task A Identify the paragraph from which each of the following statements is derived. You may choose a paragraph more than once. Each paragraph in the above text is marked with a letter.

1. People endeavored to wipe out malaria in the 1960s but failed because malaria became resistant to the medicine used at that time.

2. A number of products such as lumefantrine, piperaquine, and pyronaridine are used together with artemisinin in Project 523.

3. The paper describing artemisinin's X-ray crystal structure, pharmacology, and efficacy listed the Qinghaosu Antimalarial Coordinating Research Group as the author.

4. The follow-up wormwood studies of artemisinin only achieve 12% to 40% inhibition, which is due to a low concentration of the active ingredient.

5. Youyou Tu and her colleagues discovered the artemisinin that saved millions of people's lives around the world.

6. Malaria was an epidemic that was recorded in lots of traditional Chinese medical literature.

7. It is suggested that combination therapy of artemisinin and mefloquine should be considered to prevent the recurrence and development of resistance.

8. The tests in humans were carried out by Guoqiao Li by using the artemisinin crystals from Yunnan Institute of Drug Research.

9. The traditional methods of boiling and high-temperature extraction could damage the active ingredient of Qinghao.

10. Artemisinin provided an effective cure since the late 1990s and was especially life-saving among the world's poorest children.

Task B Work in groups to discuss the following topic and share your opinions with the class.

Traditional Chinese Medicine vs. Western Medicine

Tu Youyou's pioneering research, which earned her a Nobel Prize, played a significant role in connecting traditional Chinese medicine with Western medicine. What implications does this have for the future of global health research and practice?

Text 2 What Are Heat Shock Proteins?

Figure 5.2 Heat Shock Protein HSP70
(Source: Wikimedia website)

Heat shock proteins, or HSPs, are created with the use of heat therapies and can help your body experience improved health, performance, and recovery. Luckily, increasing HSP production through thermotherapy is easy to do—as easy as relaxing in an **infrared sauna** or layering on some clothes. Learn more about the functions of HSPs and ways to incorporate heat therapy into your life.

For anyone unfamiliar with **molecular biology**, heat shock proteins may seem a little out there. In reality, however, these **"molecular chaperones"** (as they have been nicknamed), play an enticing role in maintaining our physical, emotional, and mental health.

What Are HSPs?

HSPs are within the family of macromolecular structures, despite their tiny size. They were discovered in the early 1960s and have since opened the doors in the field of genetics and have helped the scientific and medical communities view our genetic mapping in a new light. The family of heat shock proteins was initially characterized as a highly conserved battery of genes whose expression could be induced by heat shock. HSPs

---

heat shock protein 热休克蛋白

infrared sauna 红外桑拿

molecular biology 分子生物学

molecular chaperone 分子伴侣

provide an opportunity for each organism to "up-regulate" gene expression.

There are many different classifications of HSPs, all of which are classified by their molecular weight and their specific intracellular functions. Classifications are divided into five major families, with HSP90, HSP70, HSP60, and HSP100 being the most studied. While there are many classifications, they are all referred to as "molecular chaperones", because they serve to restabilize, reorganize, and rejuvenate intercellular order.

What Do HSPs Do?

HSPs play an essential role in maintaining the efficacy of any system of organisms. An increase in HSPs within human physiology has been demonstrated to aid in the prevention of serious neurological conditions, as well as other chronic autoimmune disorders. HSPs are created when organisms are subjected to fluctuations of temperatures extreme enough to move beyond habituated temperature.

When **thermal stress** (higher or lower temperatures than what the given species is normally habituated to) is placed on organisms, something quite extraordinary happens: All of these observed organic structures begin to produce, something medical clinicians and scientists have called heat shock proteins. When HSPs are created in response to thermal stress in the external environment, they produce great benefits to the intercellular atmosphere within both small and large organisms.

thermal stress 热应力

Benefits of HSPs

Increasing the production of HSPs generates a ton of positive effects on a biological level for anyone. They may prevent disease-causing mutations, repair damaged and misfolded proteins, and also help release more natural **growth hormones**. In other words, HSPs help your body

growth hormone 生长激素

benefit from conditions that otherwise could be lethal if presented at a higher dosage. Some benefits of HSPs include: reparation of misfolded and damaged proteins, increased immune response, reduction of free radicals, faster muscle recovery and repair, heart protection, higher insulin production, etc.

Types of Heat Therapy for HSP Production

Infrared heat therapy penetrates deeper into the body than direct contact application. This heat is capable of reaching below the surface of the skin through near-infrared heat, to the body's **soft tissue** through mid-infrared, and finally into fat cells through far-infrared wavelengths. Using an infrared sauna is a great way to incorporate infrared heat into your health regimen for HSP production, as the temperature inside an infrared sauna is adjustable and averages a comfortable 100°F to 130°F, which allows you to tolerate a longer heat therapy session for more therapeutic benefits.

soft tissue 软组织

Any type of exercise where you find yourself feeling warmer or sweatier than at your rested state will kickstart the natural release of heat shock proteins. Most studies have recorded results from cardio on the body. However, studies have shown drastic changes in two types of heat shock proteins after performing **eccentric contractions** to create enough damage to the muscle tissue. This suggests you might get more release of these proteins hitting the squat rack rather than choosing the **treadmill**.

eccentric contraction 离心收缩

treadmill 跑步机

To get the most **bang for your buck** in terms of HSP release, try layering up more than usual during your next session to help reduce any cooling of your body during resting periods. A 2017 study in the *Journal of Sports Science* suggests that while subjects tested showed somewhat of an increase in HSP release on an **arm crank ergometer**, elevating core body temperature produces a

bang for the bulk 丰厚回报

arm crank ergometer 手臂曲柄测力计

higher HSP release. So, if you're looking for the slightest edge in muscle growth and improved recovery, take advantage of this easy adjustment the next time you try to increase HSP production.

While the degree of what you'll get from a hot bath (or shower) might not be the same as what you'd get from a sauna, you may be able to give your body a similar response in terms of heat shock protein release. Subjects from a 2017 study proved just that—after being immersed up to their waistline in 40℃ water for 1 hour, they saw a spike of HSP from 23% to 39%. The 16% variance was largely due to differences in total body mass and body fat percentage (leaner individuals saw a bigger increase than the others).

HSP production is an easy thing to stimulate for added health benefits in your daily life. While you might not see immediate or drastic results, incorporating heat therapy into your routine can help your body have a healthier foundation for lasting health. Before exposing yourself to heat for extended periods of time, be sure to speak to your doctor and take all safety precautions. And always remember to hydrate after sweating it out!

(Source: Clearlight Wellness website)

Exercises

Task A Decide whether the following statements are true (T) or false (F).

1. Heat shock proteins are nicknamed "molecular chaperones" because they play an enticing role in maintaining our physical, emotional, and mental health.

2. HSPs are within the family of macromolecular structures and they are large in size.

3. HSPs are created when the temperature is much higher or lower than what the given organism is normally habituated to.

CHAPTER 5 Biomedical Science

4. You can choose to run on the treadmill instead of hitting the squat rack in order to get more release of heat shock proteins whose drastic changes would pose damage to your muscle tissues.

5. You can see immediate or drastic results as soon as you use heat therapy in your routine.

Task B Choose the word or phrase which is closest in meaning to the underlined part in each sentence.

1. Learn more about the functions of HSPs and ways to <u>incorporate</u> heat therapy into your life.
   A. combine   *B.* design   *C.* suggest   *D.* create

2. The family of heat shock proteins was initially characterized as a highly conserved battery of genes whose expression could be <u>induced</u> by heat shock.
   A. persuaded   *B.* damaged   *C.* reduced   *D.* caused

3. While there are many classifications, they are all referred to as "molecular chaperones", because they serve to restabilize, reorganize, and <u>rejuvenate</u> intercellular order.
   A. form   *B.* shape   *C.* revitalize   *D.* arrange

4. HSPs are created when organisms are subjected to <u>fluctuations</u> of temperatures extreme enough to move beyond habituated temperature.
   A. changes   *B.* booms   *C.* declinations   *D.* plummets

5. However, studies have shown <u>drastic</u> changes in two types of heat shock proteins after performing eccentric contractions to create enough damage to the muscle tissue.
   A. new   *B.* severe   *C.* minor   *D.* continuing

Task C Answer the following questions based on the text.

1. What are heat shock proteins?
2. How are heat shock proteins created?
3. What benefits can heat shock proteins bring to your life?
4. What type of heat therapy can be used to increase HSP production?
5. What changes will you get from a hot bath?

Reading Tips 科技英语的句法特点（二）

1. 时态

科技英语的常用时态是一般现在时、一般过去时和现在完成时，其他时态出现的频率比较低。

一般现在时既可以用于描述经常性或习惯性的动作或状态，也可以表示客观事实或自然现象。例如：

- The engine **operates** at maximum efficiency at a temperature of 200℃.

一般过去时主要用于描述表示过去某个时间里发生的动作或状态，或过去习惯性、经常性的动作和行为。例如：

- The research team **discovered** that the previous method **was** not accurate.

现在完成时是指发生在过去的动作或状态持续到现在，或与现在的情况有联系或影响，并可能持续发生下去。例如：

- The experiment **has shown** that the new material is stronger than the previous one.

如果某一时态超越其通常所表达的时间概念，或时间与时态并不一致，那么有可能是作者想要表达不一样的思想内涵，或赋予其特殊的语用意义。时态的选择通常会受到作者自身心理和观点的影响，因而对时态选择的分析有助于理解其立场和态度。需要指出的是，would 和 should 在科技英语中通常不用于表示过去或将来时态，而是作为情态助动词出现。would 常常表示推测，should 则表示一种义务关系，语气相对委婉。例如：

- This **would** lead to the change of the experiment result.
- This requires that water **should** be properly added at the next step.

2. 语态

科技语篇侧重叙事推理，强调客观准确，往往大量使用被动语态。据统计，科技英语中使用的被动语态频率高达 1/3。被动语态对动作的发出者不做强调，也可以理解为隐去作者以使文章更加客观。与主动语态相比，被动语态用行为、活动、作用、事实等做主语，能够突出所要说明事物的特征。这一方面有助于引起读者的注意，另一方面可以提高科技文献的客观性。例如：

- The crucible **is charged with** about 175 kg of clean sodium from which the oxide coating **has been removed**, the air **is completely displaced** by passing ammonia for 10 minutes, and the pot **is heated** strongly so as to melt the sodium rapidly.

在本例中，有四处使用了被动语态，这种情况在科技英语中并不罕见。在科技英语中，被动句很少用 by 引出动作的主体，即使用到 by，一般也多是指行为方式或使用工具的情况。而汉语中的被动语态，通常由一些显著的引导词，如"被""遭""受""使"等来体现，这些词汇的使用和适用范围有限，是被动语态在汉语中不常使用的原因之一。此外，在很多情况下，英语的被动句常常可以理解成汉语的无主句。

3. 结构形态

科技语篇一般描写的是科学技术和自然现象，注重的是事实和逻辑推导，要求给出的定义、定律、定理，或描绘的概念，或叙述的生产工艺过程，都必须严谨、精确，因此经常会使用结构比较复杂的长句。

一般而言，在句子逻辑结构方面，英语长句中的主句或重点内容先出现，后再跟分句或解释的成分，或者是由总到分、由一般到特殊、由概述到细节或解释成分。有人形象地将其比喻为一种"树式"句子结构：句中有一个"主干"，主干的各成分又有相应的修饰语，作为"枝干"。例如：

- We very much regret that the 10,000 tons of wheat under Contract No. AG-3 of August 1 scheduled to be delivered by the end of October is up to this moment not dispatched in spite of the fact that you have guaranteed an early delivery in the Contract which was actually signed on this understanding.

这个结构复杂的长句的主干是 We regret that，其枝干内容丰富，主要是 regret that 后面长宾语的结构复杂。例如有宾语后置定语（scheduled to be delivered）、介词短语（under Contract No. AG-3 of August 1; by the end of October; in spite of the fact）、同位语从句（that you have guaranteed an early delivery in the Contract）和定语从句（which was actually signed on this understanding）。其中，主句带从句，从句带短语，短语带从句，环环相扣。在阅读长句的过程中，读者先要充分运用语法知识，牢牢抓住句子的主干，再条分缕析、抽丝剥茧，直至窥其全貌。

Section B Translation

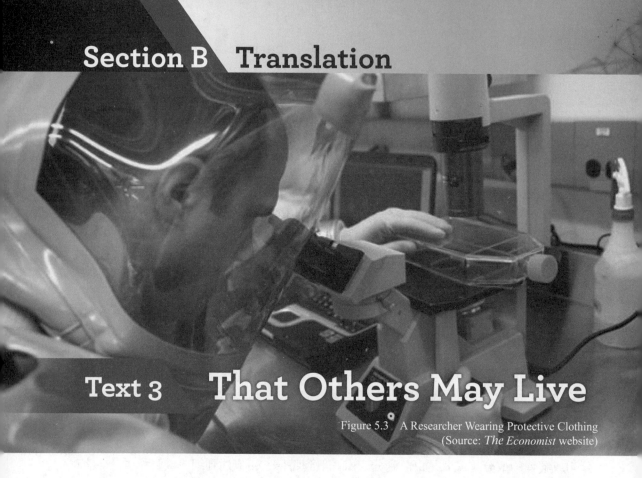

Text 3 That Others May Live

Figure 5.3   A Researcher Wearing Protective Clothing
(Source: *The Economist* website)

① It is a solemn custom in science to mark the names of collaborators who pass away during the course of an article's publication with a superscript no different than that indicating their academic affiliation. ② Very rare indeed is the case that five names on a single report should share that mark. ③ Such a report was published in *Science* this week. ④ It demonstrates the astonishing speed at which genetic sequencing can now be carried out. ⑤ At the same time, the fact that Ebola claimed five of its authors is a testament to the deadliness of the paper's subject.

On June 4th, Stephen Gire, a public health researcher at the Broad Institute in Cambridge, Massachusetts, took delivery of a polystyrene box from Kenema, Sierra Leone. Inside were vials of deactivated biological samples from 78 patients suspected to have Ebola. Mr. Gire and a colleague began to tease out the letters of each virus sample's genetic code with some of the most advanced technology yet devised for the task; before long, half of Mr. Gire's 30-strong laboratory had volunteered to help.

Then, those sequences of genetic letters were fed into a computer model that looks for hints of mutations where the letters differ. The particular mutations that separate each sample gave hints as to how closely related each was and, because mutations happen naturally at a predictable rate, how long ago they diverged from a common ancestor virus. The networks of transmission from one

CHAPTER 5 Biomedical Science

person to another were laid bare in a laboratory half a world away.

The data suggests that the virus that has now killed more than 1,400 and infected more than 3,000 arose as a distinct strain in 2004. It descended from the 1976 Zaire variant, which usually emerges in central Africa. It may have been lurking in Guinea in the interim, in the "natural reservoir"—presumed to be an animal such as a fruit bat, which can carry the virus without harm. The outbreaks in Guinea and Sierra Leone, as was suspected, appear to have emerged from a single point of contact with the reservoir, and it seems that all of the known cases in Sierra Leone stem from one group of women who attended the funeral of a traditional healer in Guinea in May.

All this insight was gleaned in record time. In all, the genetic sequencing—a quadrupling of the world's genetic knowledge of Ebola—took five days. The computational analysis took four more. Even compared to just a few years ago, that is an extraordinary pace. Mr. Gire is now working to accomplish the same wizardry in the places where the outbreaks occur. He runs a program sponsored by the World Bank to provide technological tools and training for scientists in Nigeria and Sierra Leone within the next two years.

(Source: The Economist *website)*

Exercises

Task A Review the original translation of the underlined sentences in the source text and make any necessary revisions. Then learn how to improve your revisions from the analysis and modification of the translation provided.

这篇短文是一篇科技新闻报道，主要介绍了埃博拉病毒的基因测序工作。文章开头并没有直奔主题，而是阐述了从事埃博拉病毒研究的危险性，即一些研究者在开展科研的过程中献出了宝贵的生命。译文评价如下：

原文①：It is a solemn custom in science to mark the names of collaborators who pass away during the course of an article's publication with a superscript no different than that indicating their academic affiliation.

初译①：在科学界有这样一个庄严的传统，即将在论文发表过程中逝世的科研合作者的名字以上标的形式标注出来，这个传统也无异于宣称了这些人员的学术地位。

学生评改：_____

> 评析：原文①是一个含有定语从句和比较结构的长难句，翻译时有一定的难度。其中，在处理以 no different than 为标志的比较结构时容易出现失误，容易将比较对象理解为 to mark the names of collaborators...with a superscript 和 indicating their academic affiliation。实际上，通过句法分析可以看出，二者并非并列结构，因为短语 no different than 之后并不是直接跟着 indicating their academic affiliation，而是有一个代词 that。由此可见，比较的对象应该是 a superscript 和 the superscript indicating their academic affiliation。此外，academic affiliation 是一个专业的学术表达，意为"学术机构或单位"。另外，如果译者具有较强的信息搜索意识，完全可以搜索到这篇文章的原文，那么就会清楚原文是如何对去世作者进行标记的，从而避免了盲目的翻译。因此，运用网络工具进行搜索的能力也是译者在信息时代必备的一项重要技能。
>
> 改译：在科学界有一个庄严的习俗，即如果有合作者在论文发表过程中去世，人们就会以上标的形式标记他们的名字，这种标记与表明他们所属学术机构的上标类似。

原文②③：Very rare indeed is the case that five names on a single report should share that mark. Such a report was published in *Science* this week.

初译②③：然而，在单独一篇学术报告中出现五个人名共同享有这一上标的情况实属罕见。而在本周的《科学》上就发表了这样一篇学术报告。

学生评改：_____

评析：初译②中一个明显的错误就是 share 这个单词的翻译。根据原文①可知，如果名字带有特殊的标记，那么这意味着这位作者已经去世。所以，名字上出现这种标记并非是一种荣耀，而是一种悲哀的表示。初译将 share 译为"共同享有"显然是搞错了语体色彩，原本表达消极意义的词被翻译成具有积极意义的词。另外，从整体上看，初译②基本传递了原文的概念意义，但是人际意义或情感意义却没有得到忠实的传递。从原文句子结构可以看出，这是一个倒装结构，目的是强调这种情况十分罕见，而且句子中还出现了表示强调语气的 should 一词。然而，在初译中，这些表达情感和语气的信息都没有充分地体现出来。虽然译者从汉语表达习惯出发对译文的句子结构进行了调整，但却忽略了原文的形式特征和情感意义，因此这一译法并不可取。建议按照原文的句子结构进行翻译，保持原文的强调语气。初译③与初译②的情况类似，虽然原文的意思得到了传递，但是语气不够强烈，与前文的联系也不够紧密。如果将其译为"而这样一篇报告就发表在本周的《科学》杂志上"，那么译文的接受效果将会更佳。

改译：实属罕见的是，在一篇报告中竟然同时有五位作者的名字上出现了这种标记，而这样一篇报告就发表在本周的《科学》杂志上。

原文④：It demonstrates the astonishing speed at which genetic sequencing can now be carried out.

初译④：该报告表明目前病毒基因测序工作能以惊人的速度完成。

学生评改：_____

_____

评析：此句翻译得较为妥当，语义准确、表达通顺。

原文⑤：At the same time, the fact that Ebola claimed five of its authors is a testament to the deadliness of the paper's subject.

初译⑤：在这项研究期间，埃博拉病毒带走了这五位作者的生命这一事实也证明了论文主题的致命性。

学生评改：_____

> 评析：初译⑤中出现了一个比较严重的误译，即原文中的 a testament to the deadliness of the paper's subject 被译为"证明了论文主题的致命性"。通过阅读全文可知，这篇论文的主题是基因测序，埃博拉病毒夺走五位作者生命这一事实不能说明该主题的致命性，而是说明了这篇论文研究对象（埃博拉病毒）的致命性。初译者在翻译的过程中望文生义，直接将 subject 译成"主题"，说明其对文章的理解还不够深入，或者对词汇的把握还不够全面。鉴于此，可以考虑将这句话翻译成"证明了论文研究对象的致命性"或者"证实了从事该项研究极具危险性"。之所以没有将其翻译成"证实了从事该项研究的致命性"，是因为病毒本身具有致命性，但"从事这项研究"并不致命，只可以表述为"非常危险"或"极具危险性"。
>
> 改译：与此同时，埃博拉病毒夺去五位作者生命的事实也证实了从事该项研究极具危险性。

Task B Translate the following text into Chinese.

The basic principle of gene editing involves the use of a molecular tool called the CRISPR-Cas9 system, which can precisely identify and cut DNA sequences. Scientists can use this system to delete, replace, or add specific DNA sequences, thereby altering the function of genes.

One of the major applications of gene editing is the treatment of genetic diseases. For example, it has been used to treat a genetic disorder called sickle cell anemia, which affects the production of hemoglobin in red blood cells. By using gene editing to modify the hemoglobin gene, scientists were able to produce functional red blood cells that could potentially cure the disease.

Another potential application of gene editing is in the field of cancer research. By modifying genes that are responsible for the growth and spread of cancer cells, scientists hope to develop new therapies for cancer treatment.

Despite the potential benefits of gene editing, there are also concerns about its use. One of the main ethical concerns is the potential for unintended consequences, such as the introduction of new genetic mutations that could cause harm. There are also concerns about the potential for misuse of the technology, such as the creation of "designer babies" with desired traits.

CHAPTER 5 Biomedical Science

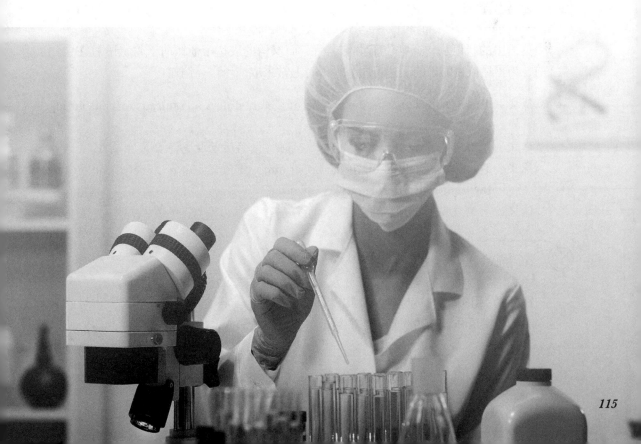

Translation Tips 状语从句的翻译方法

英语中的状语从句一般由从属连接词引导，根据功能可以分为时间状语从句、地点状语从句、原因状语从句、条件状语从句、目的状语从句、方式状语从句、让步状语从句等。状语从句的位置比较灵活，一般可以采取顺译法、倒译法、融合法和转译法。

 1. 顺译法

如果英语中的状语从句位于主句之前，和汉语中状语的位置相同，那么翻译时可以按照原文的顺序进行。例如：

原文：**When small eddies develop in Jupiter's atmosphere**, the Great Red Spot tends to suck them in.
译文：当较小的漩涡在木星的大气层中形成时，木星大红斑往往会将其吞没。

某些情况下，即使英语中的状语从句位于主句之后，也可以采取顺译法，只要按照原文的顺序翻译之后不会影响译文的通畅性和流畅性就好。例如：

原文：The material first used was copper **for the reason that it is easily obtained in its pure state**.
译文：最先使用的材料是铜，因为纯态铜容易获取。

 2. 倒译法

英语中的状语从句通常位于主句之后，而汉语的表达习惯倾向于将状语放在主句之前，为了适应目的语的表达习惯，汉译时通常采取倒译法。例如：

原文：There is no change in the motion of a body **unless a resultant force is acting on it**.
译文：除非有一个合力作用于物体，否则物体的运动状态不会发生变化。
原文：The direct exploration of the upper atmosphere didn't become possible **until the high-altitude rocket was invented**.
译文：直到发明了高空火箭后，人们才实现了对上层大气的直接探测。

 3. 融合法

在翻译英语中的方式或原因状语从句时，有时为了符合汉语的表达习惯，可将其融入主句的主语和谓语之间，将两个句子融为一体。例如：

原文：The uses of semiconductors were determined **after their properties became understood**.

译文：半导体的用途是在人们了解其性质之后才确定的。

原文：Some materials are called good conductors **because electricity goes through them well**.

译文：某些材料因导电性好而被称为良导体。

4. 转译法

转译法是指根据英语中状语从句暗含的逻辑关系，将其译成汉语中相应的其他状语从句。比如，把条件状语从句翻译成时间状语从句。例如：

原文：**If the admissible gripping force is exceeded**, a hydraulic overload protection is operated.

译文：当握持力超过允许值时，液压超负荷保护装置就会起作用。

上例中的 If the admissible gripping force is exceeded 是一个条件状语从句，在译文中转换为时间状语从句"当握持力超过允许值时"。

原文：**Where a vessel has vertical sides**, the pressure on the bottom is equal to the height of the liquid times its density.

译文：如果器壁垂直，那么容器底部压强等于液体高度乘以液体的密度。

上例中的 Where a vessel has vertical sides 是一个地点状语从句，在译文中转换为条件状语从句"如果器壁垂直"。

CHAPTER 6
Automatic Engineering

Introduction

Engineering is a vast field that involves building helpful technology and infrastructure to aid in daily life. Automation engineers look for ways to simplify activities for employees, consumers, and companies by automating certain systems. Automatic engineering is self-regulating and enables something to work or happen without being directly controlled by a person. It has a wide range of applications and branches. In this chapter, Text 1 is a passage for fast reading, dealing with drone technology; Text 2 is a passage for intensive reading, introducing 3D printing; and Text 3 is a passage for translation, discussing the robots in home and telerobots. The learning objective of this chapter is to familiarize the learners with the ways to distinguish between facts and opinions of EST and the translation techniques for attributive clauses in EST.

Lead-in Questions

1. Since automatic engineering has been there for a while, do you know anything about its latest development or its future evolution?
2. Can you brainstorm the different applications or branches of automatic engineering? What is the core technology or study in this field?

Section A Fast and Intensive Reading

Text 1 Drone Technology

Figure 6.1 Unmanned Aerial Vehicle Drones
(Source: Pixabay website)

A   Drone technology has been widely used for commercial, industrial, and military purposes. Whether you call them unmanned aerial vehicles (UAVs), miniature pilotless aircraft, or flying mini robots, drones are rapidly growing in popularity. They are still in the infancy stage in terms of mass adoption and usage, but drones have already broken through rigid traditional barriers in industries which otherwise seemed impenetrable by similar technological innovations.

B   Over the past few years, unmanned aircraft have become central to the functions of various businesses and governmental organizations and have managed to pierce through areas where certain industries were either stagnant or lagging behind. From quick deliveries at rush hour to scanning an unreachable military base, drone features are proving to be extremely beneficial in places where man cannot reach or is unable to perform in a timely and efficient manner.

C   Increasing work efficiency and productivity, decreasing workload and production costs, improving accuracy, refining service and customer relations, and resolving security issues on a vast scale are a few of the top uses drones offer industries globally. Adoption of drone technology across industries leapt from the fad stage to the mega-trend stage fairly quickly as more and more businesses started to realize its potential, scope, and scale of global reach.

CHAPTER 6 Automatic Engineering

D   Whether these unmanned aircraft are controlled by a remote or accessed via a smartphone app, they possess the capability of reaching the most remote areas with little to no manpower needed and require the least amount of effort, time, and energy. This is one of the biggest reasons why they are being adopted worldwide, especially by these four sectors: military, commercial, personal, and future technology.

E   Drones have been around for more than two decades, but their roots date back to World War I when both the U.S. and France worked on developing automatic, unmanned airplanes. But the last few years have been significant in terms of drone adoption, usage expansion across industries, and global awareness.

F   From technically-manning-sensitive military areas to luring hobbyists throughout the world, drone technology has developed and prospered in the last few years. Individuals, commercial entities, and governments have come to realize that drones have multiple useful features, which include: aerial photography for journalism and film; gathering information or supplying essentials for disaster management; thermal sensor drones for search and rescue operations; geographic mapping of inaccessible terrain and locations; law enforcement and border control surveillance; storm tracking and forecasting hurricanes and tornadoes, etc. Development of hundreds of more uses of drones is underway due to the multiple investments pouring into this promising industry every day.

G   Military usage of drones has become the primary use in today's world. Used as target decoys for combat missions, research and development, and supervision, drones have been part and parcel of the military forces worldwide. According to data from Globe Newswire, the global market size of military drones is projected to reach $23.78 billion by 2027. Military spending also tends to come in larger increments, as a single U.S. Predator drone costs approximately $4 million. UAVs will continue to be applied in various military operations due to their high convenience in reducing losses and enabling the execution of high-profile and time-sensitive missions.

H   Commercial usage of drones is gaining steady momentum and has become the talk of the hour, as multiple industries are working with drones as part of their daily regular business functions. The market size of drone services is expected to grow from $4.4 billion in 2018 to $63.6 billion by 2025.

Industries are working with drones as part of their daily business functions. The commercial drone industry has begun to see some consolidation and major investments from industrial conglomerates, chip companies, IT consulting firms, and major defense contractors. For now, the industry leaders are still a handful of early-stage manufacturers in Europe, Asia, and North America. As it becomes cheaper to customize commercial drones, the door will be opened to allow new functionality in a wide array of niche spaces.

I As the sales of the civilian drones rise, the safety concerns surrounding them among regulators and law enforcement agencies also tend to go up, seeing the past of drone collisions with airplanes and crashes into crowded stadiums. At the end of 2019, there were 990,000 recreational operators registered and an estimated 1.32 million recreational drones in the United States. And no small amount of that will come from the sale of personal drones used for film-making, recording, still photography, and gaming by common tech-savvy enthusiasts. Consumers will, however, spend $17 billion on drones over the next few years. Drones come in all shapes and sizes, from small and inexpensive single-rotor devices to large, $1,000+ quadcopters with GPS, multiple camera arrays, and first-person control.

J Drone technology is constantly evolving, so future drone technology is currently undergoing groundbreaking progressive improvement. Drone technology has seven potential generations, and the majority of current technology sits in the fifth and sixth generations. Here is the breakdown of the technology generations:

- **Generation 1:** Basic remote control aircraft of all forms.
- **Generation 2:** Static design, fixed camera mount, video recording and still photos, and manual piloting control.
- **Generation 3:** Static design, two-axis gimbals, HD video, basic safety models, and assisted piloting.
- **Generation 4:** Transformative designs, three-axis gimbals, 1080P HD video or higher-value instrumentation, improved safety modes, and autopilot modes.
- **Generation 5:** Transformative designs, 360° gimbals, 4K video or higher-value instrumentation, and intelligent piloting modes.
- **Generation 6:** Commercial suitability, safety and regulatory standards-

CHAPTER 6 Automatic Engineering

based design, platform and payload adaptability, automated safety modes, intelligent piloting models and full autonomy, and airspace awareness.

- **Generation 7:** Complete commercial suitability, fully compliant safety and regulatory standards-based design, platform and payload interchangeability, automated safety modes, enhanced intelligent piloting models and full autonomy, full airspace awareness, and auto action (takeoff, land, and mission execution).

K   The next generation of drones, Generation 7, is already underway, as 3DRobotics announced the world's first all-in-one smart drone called Solo. Smart drones with built-in safeguards and compliance technology, smart accurate sensors, and self-monitoring are the next big revolution in drone technology that would provide new opportunities in transport, military, logistics, and commercial sectors. As these technologies continue to evolve and grow, drones will become safer and more dependable.

(Source: Business Insider website)

Notes

conglomerate: a large company formed by joining together different firms 联合公司；企业集团

decoy: a thing or a person that is used to trick somebody into doing what you want them to do, going where you want them to go, etc.   诱饵；诱惑物

defense contractor: the arms industry, a global business that manufactures and sells weapons and military technology and equipment   国防承包商

gimbal: a pivoting device for keeping instruments (e.g., a compass) horizontal in a moving ship, etc.   平衡环，水平环

quadcopter: Also called a quadrotor helicopter or quadrotor, it is a multirotor helicopter that is lifted and propelled by four rotors.   四轴飞行器（又称四旋翼、四转子，一种多轴飞行器）

Exercises

Task A **Identify the paragraph from which each of the following statements is derived. You may choose a paragraph more than once. Each paragraph in the above text is marked with a letter.**

1. The commercial drone industry leaders are mainly in Asia, North America, and Europe.

2. Drones can be traced back to World War I.

3. There was a giant leap of drone adoption from a fad to a big trend.

4. We are currently in between Generation 5 and Generation 6 of drone technology.

5. Drone technology is still in the initial stage in terms of mass adoption and usage.

6. There will be hundreds of more uses of drones coming out due to the inpouring of investments.

7. There have been growing concerns over personal drone safety among regulators and law enforcement agencies.

8. Last few years witnessed that drones became the central to the functions of businesses and governmental organizations.

9. Of all the uses, the most important usage of drones is in military currently.

10. One big reason for the popularity of drones is their capability of reaching remote areas with little manpower needed.

Task B **Work in groups to discuss the following topic and share your opinions with the class.**

How Are Drones Shaping Our Future?

Drones have become a common sight in our daily life, and some companies have recently used them to offer food delivery services to their clients. What are some unexplored and creative uses of drone technology, and how might they shape our society and routines in the coming years?

Text 2

3D Printing: What You Need to Know

Figure 6.2 A Statue Produced by Using 3D Technique
(Source: CPACanada website)

3D printers have become affordable enough to hit the mainstream, but should you buy one? Here's what to consider—about materials, possible uses, software, and much more—before you dive in.

They're not your granddad's **daisy wheel printer**, or your mom's dot matrix. In fact, they bear little resemblance to today's document or photo printers, which can only print in boring, old two dimensions. As their name suggests, 3D printers can build three-dimensional objects, out of a variety of materials. They're going mainstream, showing up at retailers such as Staples, Best Buy, and Home Depot, and you can buy numerous 3D printers and their supplies on Amazon.com and through other online outlets. Though still mostly found on shop floors or in design studios, in schools and community centers, and in the hands of hobbyists, 3D printers are increasingly being found on workbenches, in **rec rooms**, and kitchens—and perhaps in a home near you, if not your own.

At its most basic, 3D printing is a manufacturing process in which material is laid down, layer by layer, to form a three-dimensional object. (This is deemed an

daisy wheel printer 菊轮打印机

rec room 娱乐室（美语）

additive process because the object is built from scratch, as opposed to subtractive processes in which material is cut, drilled, milled, or machined off.) Although 3D printers employ a variety of materials (such as plastic or metal) and techniques, they share the ability to turn digital files containing three-dimensional data—whether created on a **computer-aided design** (CAD) or computer-aided manufacturing (CAM) program, or from a 3D scanner—into physical objects.

> computer-aided design 计算机辅助设计

3D printing can be considered printing, although not as it's traditionally been defined. The relevant Webster's definitions of "printing" center on the production of printed matter, publications, or photographs, and producing by means of impression (the application of pressure). Neither definition really fits 3D printing. But from a technological perspective, 3D printing is an outgrowth of traditional printing, in which a layer of material (usual ink) is applied. Usually, it's so thin that there is no noticeable height (though with solid ink printers, it is somewhat thicker). What 3D printing does is to greatly extend that height through the application of multiple layers. So it would make sense to expand the definition of printing to include the fabrication of three-dimensional objects in this manner.

Much like traditional printers, 3D printers use a variety of technologies. The most commonly known is fused deposition modeling (FDM), also known as fused filament fabrication (FFF). In it, a filament is melted and deposited through a heated extrusion nozzle in layers. The first 3D printers to come to market, made in the mid-1990s by Stratasys with help from IBM, used FDM (a term trademarked by Stratasys), as do most 3D printers geared to consumers, hobbyists, and schools.

Another technology used in 3D printing is **stereolithography**. In it, a UV laser is shined into a vat of

> stereolithography 立体平板打印

ultraviolet-sensitive photopolymer, tracing the object to be created on its surface. The polymer solidifies wherever the beam touches it, and the beam "prints" the object layer by layer per the instructions in the CAD or CAM file it's working from.

In a variation on that, you also have **digital light projector** (DLP) 3D printing. This method exposes a liquid polymer to light from a digital light processing projector. This hardens the polymer layer by layer until the object is built, and the remaining liquid polymer is drained off.

digital light projector 数字光投影技术

Multi-jet modeling is an inkjet-like 3D printing system that sprays a colored, glue-like binder onto successive layers of powder where the object is to be formed. This is among the fastest methods, and one of the few that support multi-color printing. It's possible to modify a standard inkjet to print with materials other than ink. Enterprising do-it-yourselfers have built or modded print heads, generally piezoelectric heads, to work with various materials—in some cases printing out the print heads themselves on other 3D printers! Companies like MicroFab Technologies sell 3D-capable print heads (as well as complete printing systems).

multi-jet modeling 多喷嘴成型技术

Selective laser sintering (SLS) uses a high-powered laser to fuse particles of plastic, metal, ceramic, or glass. At the end of the job, the remaining material is recycled. Electron beam melting (EBM) uses—you guessed it—an electron beam to melt metal powder, layer by layer. Titanium is often used with EBM to synthesize medical implants, as well as aircraft parts.

selective laser sintering 选择性激光烧结法

Depending on the technique, 3D printers can use a variety of materials, including but not limited to metals (stainless steel, solder, aluminum, and titanium among them); plastics and polymers (including composites that combine plastics with metals, wood, and other materials); ceramics; plaster; glass; and even foodstuffs like cheese, icing, and chocolate!

With 3D printing, designers have the ability to quickly turn concepts into 3D models or prototypes (a.k.a. "rapid prototyping") and implement rapid design changes. It lets manufacturers produce products on demand rather than in large runs, improving inventory management and reducing warehouse space. People in remote locations can fabricate objects that would otherwise be inaccessible to them.

From a practical standpoint, 3D printing can save money and material versus subtractive techniques, as very little raw material is wasted. And it promises to change the nature of manufacturing, eventually letting consumers download files for printing even complex 3D objects—including, for example, electronics devices—in their own homes.

(Source: PCMag website)

Exercises

Task A Decide whether the following statements are true (T) or false (F).

1. Unlike traditional printers, 3D printers can build three-dimensional objects, out of a variety of materials.

2. The traditional techniques, such as cutting, drilling, milling, and machining off, could be used in 3D printing.

3. Although 3D printers employ a variety of materials (such as plastics or metals), they share the same technique.

4. Multi-jet modeling is among the fastest 3D printing methods, and one of the few that support multi-color printing.

5. 3D printing can save money and materials versus subtractive techniques.

CHAPTER 6 Automatic Engineering

Task B Choose the word or phrase which is closest in meaning to the underlined part in each sentence.

1. In fact, they bear little <u>resemblance</u> to today's document or photo printers, which can only print in boring, old two dimensions.
   A. feature   B. comparison   C. likeness   D. difference

2. So it would make sense to expand the definition of printing to include the <u>fabrication</u> of three-dimensional objects in this manner.
   A. extension   B. production   C. copying   D. recreation

3. Multi-jet modeling is an inkjet-like 3D printing system that sprays a colored, glue-like binder onto <u>successive</u> layers of powder where the object is to be formed.
   A. consecutive   B. following   C. intermittent   D. approximate

4. Titanium is often used with EBM to <u>synthesize</u> medical implants, as well as aircraft parts.
   A. process   B. collect   C. analyze   D. combine

5. With 3D printing, designers have the ability to quickly turn concepts into 3D models or prototypes (a.k.a. "rapid prototyping") and <u>implement</u> rapid design changes.
   A. enhance   B. speed up   C. carry out   D. complement

Task C Answer the following questions based on the text.

1. What is 3D printing?
2. What are the frequently-used technologies in 3D printing?
3. How does the digital light projector 3D printing work?
4. What materials can be used in 3D printing?
5. What are the benefits of 3D printing?

Reading Tips 事实与观点的区别

科技语篇的核心内容由事实（fact）和观点（opinion）组成。事实是客观存在和发生的事情，或是可以证明的事情和真相，讲求客观的证据。比如，"The Earth is round."这一事实可以通过卫星图像等科学手段进行证明。而观点是个人的判断、信仰或感觉，个人认为是正确的，但并不能确定（not certain about）是否真的正确。比如，"The best type of pizza is made with a thin crust."这一说法是一种观点，因为没有客观证据证明它是真是假。事实与观点有时并不容易分辨，因为观点常常是基于事实或部分事实的。下面分别介绍事实类和观点类表述的语言特征。

 1. 事实类表述的语言特征

（1）中性语气

事实类表述通常以客观、中性的语气呈现，不存在任何个人倾向或情绪。在科技语篇中，作者在陈述事实时通常比较直白，且不带感情色彩。例如：

- The Earth is part of a solar system that includes eight planets and numerous other celestial bodies, such as asteroids and comets.
- The process of evolution through natural selection has shaped the diversity of life on the Earth over billions of years.

（2）确定性表达

为了增强所述事实的可信性，科技语篇在陈述事实时会使用一些表达确定性的句式，如 it has been proven that、it is a well-known fact that、it is an established truth that 等。当句子中存在类似表达时，该句子则很可能是事实。例如：

- **It has been confirmed that** drinking green tea can help lower cholesterol levels.
- **It is well established that** the human body requires a balanced diet in order to function properly.

（3）术语和数据支持

技术文本通常需要使用大量专业术语和词汇，以准确传达信息。如果科技语篇中的某一陈述使用了专业术语，或者有数据支持，那么这一陈述则很有可能是事实。例如：

- **The laws of thermodynamics** govern the relationships between energy and heat in physical systems.
- According to a report by the World Health Organization, there were **229 million cases** of malaria worldwide in 2019.

2. 观点类表述的语言特征

（1）评价性表达

个人观点通常用于表达对事实的评价、看法或意见等，因此在表述时会不可避免地使用一些评价性词汇或短语。在科技英语中，常见的评价性词汇包括 promising、insufficient、valuable、unsatisfactory、state-of-the-art 等，评价性的短语或句式包括 show great potential、still have room for improvement、have been widely adopted in the field 等。例如：

- Although this technology has shown **promising** results, it still has **limitations** that need to be addressed.
- Swarms of ants can do many **difficult** tasks, but ants aren't **clever** architects or soldiers.

（2）不确定性表达

在表述个人观点时，作者在很多情况下会使用一些表达不确定意义的修饰词，如 probably、likely、seem 等。类似的表达还包括情态动词 might、may、could 等，副词 perhaps、possibly、maybe、probably、theoretically 等，量词 some、many、most of 等，以及结构化表达，如 it is possible that、it is conceivable that、no one knows for certain that 等。例如：

- **There is a possibility that** this approach **may** not work for all cases.
- The new technology will **probably** revolutionize the industry in the next decade.

（3）观点性表达

当句子以 I believe、I think、in my opinion 这一类表示观点性的词汇或短语开头时，很明显这是作者在表达自己的个人观点，而不是在陈述事实。类似的词汇和短语还包括 suggest、indicate、argue for 等，它们既可以以主动的形式出现，也可以以被动的形式出现，如 it is considered/believed/suspected that 等。例如：

- **This suggests that** some ants wait for the other ants to find a food source for them.
- **It is believed that** the cause of the disease is still unknown.

很多情况下，科技语篇中的观点与事实是交织在一起的，呈现出一种"你中有我，我中有你"的状态，阅读时读者需要结合语境进行综合判断。区分事实与观点不仅可以帮助读者更加全面、准确地把握语篇信息和意图，而且有助于培养其批判性思维和独立思考的能力。

Section B Translation

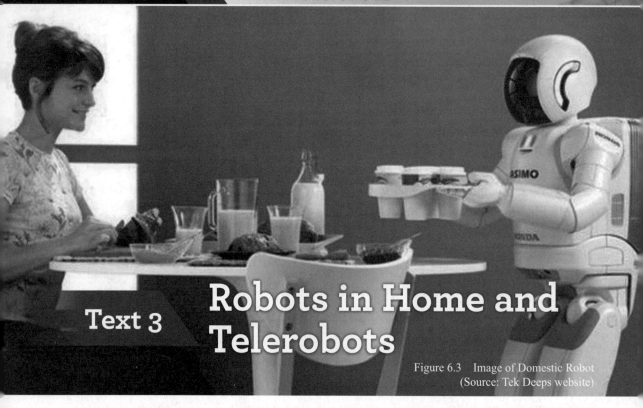

Text 3 **Robots in Home and Telerobots**

Figure 6.3 Image of Domestic Robot
(Source: Tek Deeps website)

Robots in Home

As their price falls, and their performance and computational ability rises, making them both affordable and sufficiently autonomous, robots are increasingly being seen in the home where they are taking on simple but unwanted jobs, such as vacuum cleaning, floor cleaning, and lawn mowing. While they have been on the market for several years, 2006 saw a great increase in the number of domestic robots sold. By 2006, iRobot had sold more than two million vacuuming robots. They tend to be relatively autonomous, usually only requiring a command to begin their job. They then proceed to go about their business in their own way. At such, they display a good deal of agency, and are considered intelligent robots.

Telerobots

① When a human cannot be present on site to perform a job because it is dangerous, far away, or inaccessible, teleoperated robots, or telerobots are used. ② Rather than following a predetermined sequence of movements, a telerobot is controlled from a distance by a human operator. ③ The robot may be in another room or another country, or may be on a very different scale to the operator. ④ A laparoscopic surgery robot allows the

CHAPTER 6 Automatic Engineering

surgeon to work inside a human patient on a relatively small scale compared to open surgery, significantly shortening recovery time.

⑤ An interesting use of a telerobot is by the author Margaret Atwood, who has recently started using a robot pen to sign books remotely. ⑥ At the other end of the spectrum, iRobot ConnectR robot is designed to be used by anyone to stay in touch with family or friends from far away. ⑦ Still another robot is being used by doctors to communicate with patients, allowing the doctor to be anywhere in the world. ⑧ This increased the number of patients a doctor can monitor.

(Source: Google website)

Exercises

Task A Review the original translation of the underlined sentences in the source text and make any necessary revisions. Then learn how to improve your revisions from the analysis and modification of the translation provided.

这篇短文主要介绍了两种不同类型的智能机器人：家用机器人和遥控机器人。译文评价如下：

> 原文①：When a human cannot be present on site to perform a job because it is dangerous, far away, or inaccessible, teleoperated robots, or telerobots are used.
>
> 初译①：当人类因危险、遥远或无法到达而无法在现场进行作业时，就会使用远程操作机器人或遥控机器人。

学生评改：_____

_____

> 评析：初译①有三处翻译不够准确。第一处在于初译中"危险、遥远或无法到达"这几个形容词的描述对象不够明确，原文中 dangerous、far away 和 inaccessible 修饰的限定对象是 it，也就是 a job，而初译的处理方式过于简单。建议根据汉语的表达习惯，采用四字短语的表达方式使之更加明确，如"工作危险、距离遥远、无法接近"。第二处在于译文"就会使

133

用远程操作机器人或遥控机器人"这句话缺少主语。虽然这种说法在口语中可以接受，而且通过上下文很容易得知主语是"人们"，但在书面语中要尽量避免缺少主语的情况。解决这个问题方法有两种：一种是将从句中的"人类"省略，在此处增加主语"人们"；另一种是将"遥控机器人"作为主语，改为"遥控机器人就派上用场了"。第三处仍与这句话有关，即译文存在歧义，读者可能会理解成"远程操作机器人"和"遥控机器人"是两种不同类型的机器人。实际上，从原文可以得知二者是同一事物，只不过后者是简写而已，因此可以考虑将其放在括号中，以表明二者的关系。

改译：当工作危险、距离遥远、无法接近等原因使人们无法在现场开展工作时，远程操控机器人（遥控机器人）就派上用场了。

原文②：Rather than following a predetermined sequence of movements, a telerobot is controlled from a distance by a human operator.

初译②：遥控机器人并非按照预先设定的程序进行工作，而是由操作员从远处控制。

学生评改：_____

评析：此句翻译得较为妥当，语义准确、表达通顺。

原文③④：The robot may be in another room or another country, or may be on a very different scale to the operator. A laparoscopic surgery robot allows the surgeon to work inside a human patient on a relatively small scale compared to open surgery, significantly shortening recovery time.

初译③④：这些机器人可能与操作者不在一个房间，不在一个国家，也可能与操作者存在着非常不同的规模差异。与开腹手术相比，腹腔镜手术机器人使外科医生能在患者体内进行尽可能小的操作，大大缩短了恢复时间。

CHAPTER 6　Automatic Engineering

学生评改：_____
_____
_____
_____

> **评析**：原文③的翻译难度主要在于 scale 这个词，因为它的词义非常多，如"规模""等级""刻度""比例"等，但这些都不符合此处的语境。初译将其处理为"规模差异"并不恰当，因为根据原文③前半句可知，机器人可能与操作者处于不同的房间、不同的国家，而这些都属于空间范畴，从 or 这一并列连词可知后半句出现的应该是同类型类比。另外，原文④中列举的 A laparoscopic surgery robot 就是对这种情况的解释，即有的机器人可以在患者体内较小的"空间范围"里进行操作，从而缩短了患者恢复的时间。鉴于此，此处应对 scale 这个单词的词义进行引申，将其翻译为"空间尺度"或"空间范围"。
>
> **改译**：机器人可能与操作员处于不同的房间、不同的国家，甚至是截然不同的空间尺度。与开放式手术相比，腹腔镜手术机器人可以使外科医生在患者体内进行微创手术，从而大大缩短了恢复时间。

> **原文⑤**：An interesting use of a telerobot is by the author Margaret Atwood, who has recently started using a robot pen to sign books remotely.
>
> **初译⑤**：作家玛格丽特·阿特伍德（Margaret Atwood）对遥控机器人有一个有趣的应用，她最近开始使用机器笔来远程签名。

学生评改：_____
_____

> **评析**：由于英汉两种语言在表达方式上存在较大差异，很多情况下译者需要对译文进行不同程度的调整和变通，才能使其读上去通顺、自然。如果完全照搬原文，那么译文有可能会比较拗口。初译⑤就存在这样的问题，译文"作家玛格丽特·阿特伍德（Margaret Atwood）对遥控机器人有一个有趣的应用"是完全对照原文 An interesting use of a telerobot is by the

135

author Margaret Atwood 的翻译，但这种表述显然不符合汉语的表达习惯，读上去也是晦涩难懂。其中，初译将 interesting use 处理为"有趣的应用"并不准确，改译为"妙用"则更贴近原文的意思。下一个小句中的"远程签名"的翻译也不够明确，其确切的意思应该是指"远程签名售书"。

改译：最近，作家玛格丽特·阿特伍德（Margaret Atwood）发现了远程机器人的一种妙用，她开始使用机器人笔远程签名售书。

原文⑥：At the other end of the spectrum, iRobot ConnectR robot is designed to be used by anyone to stay in touch with family or friends from far away.

初译⑥：另一方面，iRobot ConnectR 机器人被设计成任何人都可以使用来与远方的家人或朋友保持联系。

学生评改：_____

_____

评析：总体来看，初译⑥基本上传递了原文的主要信息，但表述内容有待润色。首先，原文中 At the other end of the spectrum 的字面意思是"在另一个极端"，译文处理为"另一方面"基本可以接受。但是由于前文没有提及"一方面"，这里突然出现"另一方面"会显得比较突兀。其次，科技英语中习惯使用被动语态，而汉语中并不多见。初译保留了被动语态，但读着冗余、拗口，可以考虑将被动语态转换为主动语态，采用词性转换的策略将动词词组 is designed to 转变为名词词组"设计目的"或"设计宗旨"，从而避免因被动语态而导致的语句不通顺。

改译：另外一款 iRobot ConnectR 机器人的设计宗旨在于帮助相距遥远的家人和朋友保持联系。

原文⑦⑧：Still another robot is being used by doctors to communicate with patients, allowing the doctor to be anywhere in the world.

> This increased the number of patients a doctor can monitor.
>
> 初译⑦⑧：还有一种机器人被医生用来与病人沟通，让医生可以在世界任何地方来了解病人情况。这增加了每个医生可以看护的病人数量。

学生评改：_____
_____
_____
_____

> 评析：原文⑦的翻译极有可能出现偏差：一种理解是"无论医生在世界上什么地方都可以给患者看病"；另一种理解是"无论患者在世界上什么地方，医生都可以给他们看病"。实际上，这两种可能性都存在，但上述的表述都存在以偏概全的风险。因此，最佳的处理方式是采取直译的方式，如"这使医生可以出现在世界上任何地方"。但通过上下文可以得知，这里的意思不是指"医生真的能够出现在世界上任何地方"，而是指"通过遥控机器人远程看护病人，这使医生仿佛到了世界各地"。因此，这里的"出现"应该加上双引号，以表示其具有特殊含义，并非真正的出现。此外，原文⑧和原文⑦有明显的因果关系，即得益于遥控机器人，医生可以监护病人的数量大大增加。因此，这两句可以采取合译的方式，通过增加关联词来合并翻译。
>
> 改译：此外，还有一种机器人可以用于医患交流，它可以让医生"出现"在世界上的任何地方，从而增加了他们可以监护的病人数量。

Task B Translate the following text into Chinese.

A new prosthetic hand: Its fingers are made of rigid tubes connected by soft joints. These are similarly connected to a 3D-printed plastic palm. The whole is covered with a flexible elastomer layer to mimic skin and is attached to the user's residual limb via a customized plastic socket. In contrast to current models, which are electrically powered, the new prosthetic hand is powered pneumatically by a pump held in a waist bag, with the connecting airlines running under the user's clothes alongside communication cables. The hand uses similar signal-processing algorithms to other prosthetics in the market. The big advance is that it does not require invasive surgery or electronic implants into the residual limb to communicate with the user's brain. Sensors on the skin record electrical activity from the remaining arm muscles. In an intact arm, this activity would tell those muscles how to operate the hand. Instead, they are interpreted by pattern-recognition software that sends appropriate commands to the pump to move the artificial hand in the same way. Meanwhile, other signals travel in the opposite direction from sensors in the hand's fingertips to nerves in the arm, whence they are relayed to the brain and provide a sensation of touch. The upshot is something which responds like a hand and feels like one to the user.

Translation Tips 定语从句的翻译方法

定语从句是科技英语中使用频率最高、也是最复杂的一类从句。它大致可以分为限制性定语从句（restrictive attributive clause）和非限制性定语从句（non-restrictive attributive clause）两种，前者主要起修饰限定的作用，后者则主要起补充说明的作用。虽然从形式结构上看定语从句主要是用作定语，但实际上其功能十分强大，可以充当很多其他的句子成分、分句，甚至是独立的句子。相应地，定语从句的翻译方法就非常灵活。总体而言，定语从句的翻译方法可以概括为以下三种。

 1. 翻译成"的"字短语

如果定语从句较短，且主要作用是修饰限定先行词，那么就可以直接将其翻译为汉语"的"字结构并前置做定语。例如：

原文：A conductor is a substance **which is able to carry electrons easily**.
译文：导体是一种易于携带电子的物体。
原文：The reader **who is impatient to get on to digital systems** should realize that many digital systems also require analog technology to function.
译文：对于迫切想要了解数字系统的读者来说，他们应该认识到许多数字系统的运行也需要模拟技术。

 2. 翻译成其他从句

英语中的定语从句形式多样，语义变化丰富而又含蓄。尽管从句法角度来看，定语从句和主句之间是修饰限定关系，但在很多情况下定语从句可以在特定语境中充当不同的句子成分，呈现不同的逻辑意义。因此，译者在翻译时可以根据具体语境将定语从句灵活转换为其他类型的从句。例如：

原文：There is another reason **why alternating current is preferred to direct current for long-distance transmission**.
译文：为什么远距离输电时交流电优于直流电，还有一个理由。（译为主语从句）
原文：Recent scientific innovations point to a future **where tiny amounts of electricity will run superfast computers**.
译文：最近的科学创新表明，未来极少的电量就足以运行超高速计算机。（译为宾语从句）
原文：Microwaves, **which have a higher frequency than ordinary radio waves**, are used routinely in sending thousands of telephone calls and television programs across a long distance.

译文：微波比一般无线电波有更高的频率，因此常用于远距离电话和电视信号传送。（译为状语从句）

原文：This is called non-linear editing, as opposed to linear editing, **in which a video has to be edited in sequence**.

译文：这被称为非线性编辑，与之相对的是线性编辑，即一段视频材料必须按时序编辑。（译为同位语从句）

原文：The turbines drive the dynamos **which generate the electricity**.

译文：涡轮机驱动发电机发电。（译为汉语兼语句）

 3. 翻译成独立句

译者还可以采取分译法将定语从句翻译为一个独立完整的单句，这种方法在非限制性定语从句的翻译中十分常见。例如：

原文：The moist atmosphere makes iron rust rapidly, **which leads us to think that water is the influence causing the corrosion**.

译文：潮湿的空气会使铁很快生锈，这会使我们认为水是引起腐蚀的原因。

原文：Nanotechnology has been described as a key manufacturing technology of the 21st century, **which will be able to manufacture almost any chemically stable structure at a low cost**.

译文：纳米技术被认为是21世纪一门重要的制造技术，它能够以较低的成本制造出几乎所有的化学成分稳定的结构。

CHAPTER 7
Artificial Intelligence

Introduction

In 1955, John McCarthy coined the term "artificial intelligence" (AI), meaning "the science and engineering of making intelligent machines". Today, it is also the name of the academic field which studies how to create computers and computer software that is capable of intelligent behavior. Major AI researchers define this field as "the study and design of intelligent agents", in which an intelligent agent is a system that perceives its environment and takes actions that maximize its chances of success. In this chapter, Text 1 is a passage for fast reading, dealing with the future development of information technology (IT) and AI; Text 2 is a passage for intensive reading, introducing augmented reality and virtual reality; and Text 3 is a passage for translation, discussing the technology of radio frequency identification. The learning objective of this chapter is to familiarize the learners with the principles of information construction of EST and the translation techniques for complex and compound sentences in EST.

Lead-in Questions

1. Most examples of AI that you hear about today from chess-playing computers to self-driving cars rely heavily on deep learning and natural language processing. Do you reckon that AI will replace us or augment our abilities to make us better at what we do?

2. The principal limitation of AI is to learn from the data. There is no other way in which knowledge can be incorporated. That means any inaccuracies in the data will be reflected in the results. Can you think of any potential risks associated with the use of AI?

Section A Fast and Intensive Reading

Text 1: The Future of Information Technology and Artificial Intelligence

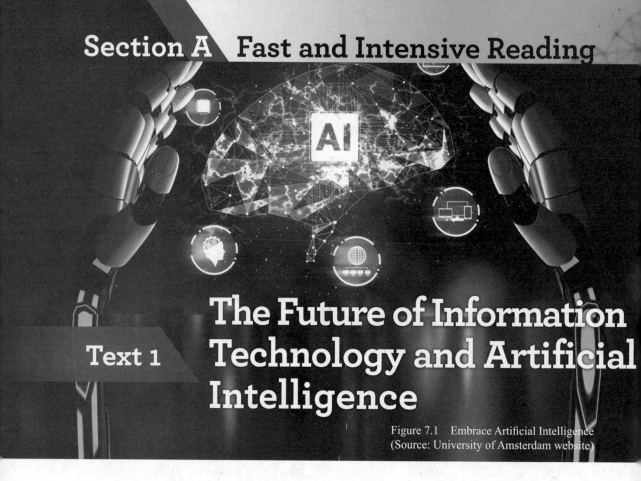

Figure 7.1　Embrace Artificial Intelligence
(Source: University of Amsterdam website)

A　Artificial intelligence has become an important aspect of the future. This applies equally as well to information technology as it does to many other industries that rely on it. Just a decade ago, AI technology seemed like something straight out of science fiction; today, we use it in everyday life without realizing it—from intelligence research to facial recognition and speech recognition to automation. AI and machine learning (ML) have taken over traditional computing methods, changing how many industries perform and conduct their day-to-day operations.

B　AI and related technologies have had a positive impact on the way the IT sector works. To put it simply, artificial intelligence is a branch of computer science that looks to turning computers into intelligent machines that would, otherwise, not be possible without direct human intervention. By making use of computer-based training and advanced algorithms, AI and MI can be used to create systems capable of mimicking human behaviors, provide solutions to difficult and complicated problems, and further develop simulations, aiming to become human-level AI.

C　According to the statistics, the AI market is expected to reach $190 billion

CHAPTER 7 Artificial Intelligence

by 2025. By 2021, global spending on cognitive and AI systems will reach $57.6 billion, while 75% of enterprise apps will use AI technology. In terms of national GDPs, AI is expected to boost China by 26.1% and the United States by 14.5% by 2030. Similarly, some 61% of business professionals point to AI and ML as their most significant data initiative over the coming year. In addition, some 95% of business executives who are skilled in using big data also use AI technology.

D   There are plenty of ways that organizations can integrate artificial intelligence into their operations. One of the most common reasons is to optimize the company's processes. Say, for instance, AI can be used to send out automatic reminders to departments, team members, and customers. It can also be used to monitor network traffic, as well as handle a wide variety of mundane and repetitive tasks that would, otherwise, eat up a lot of people's time. This, in turn, will free them up to focus their time and energy on more critical aspects of the business. But for many companies, however, the prospect of implementing AI may seem challenging and unfamiliar. In fact, roughly 37% of executives say that the main obstacle in implementing AI in their organizations is that the managers don't understand how emerging technologies work.

E   One major reason why some organizations are reluctant in implementing artificial intelligence technology is that they fear that it will make many jobs irrelevant and obsolete. These expressed concerns that "robots" will take over humans are not totally unfounded as there are certain jobs that are better handled by advanced AI, particularly when the tasks require the analysis of massive data sets. Superintelligent AI has been used to perform some tasks faster and more effectively than the human brain ever could, largely because machines don't need frequent rest periods.

F   It is, nevertheless, important to keep in mind that this is not the first time in history when technology has resulted in the loss of certain jobs. However, these job losses have always been covered by the creation of new jobs, sometimes, in fields that didn't exist before. While it's next to impossible to predict the future of artificial intelligence with any high degree of accuracy, it's relatively safe to say that the appearance and proliferation of the technology has followed a similar trend. It's because of AI that there are now a plethora of new jobs in both existing and pioneering fields.

G   That said, AI will not outperform humans, as some may believe when it comes to some specific tasks that demand human intelligence and emotions. This is why it's critical that information technology supports artificial intelligence. In more ways than one, AI works as a complement, not a replacement for the IT department. If we are to look in the not-so-distant past, many feared that self-driving cars will replace all truck drivers. More recently, however, the former CEO of Uber have said that self-driving cars will not surpass humans. The main reason is that this type of technology will never be able to handle all the driving conditions as well as human drivers can. When it comes to some exceptional conditions such as unfavorable weather conditions or traffic congestion, human drivers are still better suited to drive vehicles than AI.

H   The digital transformation and adoption of AI technology by industries has given rise to new advancements to solve and optimize many core challenges in the IT industry. Among all tech applications, AI sits at the core of development for almost every industry, with information technology being among the first. The integration of AI systems has helped reduce the burden on developers by improving efficiency, enhancing productivity, and assuring quality. If the development and deployment of IT systems at large scale were next to impossible, through AI's development of advanced algorithmic functions this is now possible.

I   Aside from using AI in software testing and development, we've touched upon, the technology can also be used together with IT in many ways, such as in service management by tracking user behavior and making suggestions and in developing computer vision (CV) technology that can be used to automate the visual understanding from a sequence of images, PDFs, videos, and text images with the help of ML algorithms.

J   Machine learning and deep learning capabilities of AI will allow systems to analyze a request submitted to a service desk. AI will find all concurrent requests, compare the newly submitted ones with those that have been previously resolved, and get an instant understanding based on past experience. The end result will be a solution to the request.

K   All in all, AI being such a powerful business tool, it can assist IT professionals in their operational processes, by providing them with a more strategic approach. By being able to track and analyze user behavior, the AI system will

CHAPTER 7 Artificial Intelligence

provide suggestions for process optimization and even help with developing a comprehensive business strategy.

(Source: My Computer Career website)

Notes

algorithm: a set of steps that are followed in order to solve a mathematical problem or to complete a computer process （数学或计算机的）运算法则

computer vision: a field that includes methods for acquiring, processing, analyzing, and understanding images and, in general, high-dimensional data from the real world in order to produce numerical or symbolic information, e.g., in the form of decisions 计算机视觉

machine learning: a subfield of computer science that evolves from the study of pattern recognition and computational learning theory in artificial intelligence 机器学习

Exercises

Task A **Identify the paragraph from which each of the following statements is derived. You may choose a paragraph more than once. Each paragraph in the above text is marked with a letter.**

1. Of all the industries, the impact of artificial intelligence on information technology is the most significant.

2. Artificial intelligence can analyze requests for service with its machine learning and deep learning capabilities.

3. The reluctance to adopt artificial intelligence lies mainly in the fear that it will take over humans.

4. Artificial intelligence is futuristic and changing many industries' performance.

5. The majority of enterprise apps use artificial intelligence technology and it can greatly boost national GDP growth.

6. Artificial intelligence can be used in many ways, but many company leaders still have concerns about its implementation in practice.

7. Artificial intelligence is a subset of computer science which tries to make computers more intelligent.

8. Information technology and artificial intelligence can work together in developing computer vision technology.

9. Artificial intelligence will not replace information technology because it works to complement information technology rather than take its place.

10. Technology may lead to job losses, but it also means the creation of new jobs in new fields.

Task B Work in groups to discuss the following topic and share your opinions with the class.

ChatGPT: Promises or Threats?

Debate surrounds the impact of ChatGPT language models, with some proponents claiming benefits for people and others suggesting the potential for harm. On the one hand, there are proponents of AI language models who argue that GPT can bring numerous benefits to society; on the other hand, there are those who fear that GPT could potentially have destructive consequences for humanity. Where do you stand on this issue?

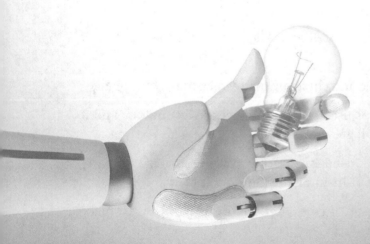

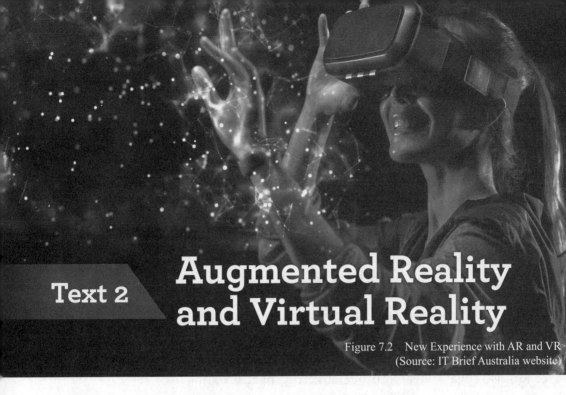

Text 2: Augmented Reality and Virtual Reality

Figure 7.2 New Experience with AR and VR
(Source: IT Brief Australia website)

Augmented reality and **virtual reality** (commonly abbreviated as AR and VR respectively) are reality technologies that either enhance or replace a real-life environment with a simulated one. Augmented reality augments your surroundings by adding digital elements to a live view, often by using the camera on a smartphone. Virtual reality is a completely immersive experience that replaces a real-life environment with a simulated one.

augmented reality 增强现实
virtual reality 虚拟现实

In AR, a virtual environment is designed to coexist with the real environment, with the goal of being informative and providing additional data about the real world, which a user can access without having to do a search. For example, industrial AR apps could offer instant **troubleshooting information** when a handset is aimed at a piece of failing equipment. Virtual reality encompasses a complete environmental simulation that replaces the user's world with an entirely virtual world. Because these virtual environments are entirely fabricated, they are often designed to be larger than life. For example, VR could let a user box with a cartoon version of Mike Tyson in a virtual boxing ring.

troubleshooting information
故障排除信息

While both virtual reality and augmented reality are

designed to bring a simulated environment to the user, each concept is unique and involves different use cases. In addition to entertainment scenarios, augmented reality is also increasingly being used by businesses, because of its ability to generate informational overlays that add useful, real-world scenarios. We'll delve into how both of these reality technologies work, with a specific focus on the business cases for AR, in the sections that follow.

While both technologies involve simulated reality, AR and VR rely on different underlying components and generally serve different audiences. In virtual reality, the user almost always wears an eye-covering headset and headphones to completely replace the real world with the virtual one. The idea of VR is to eliminate the real world as much as possible and **insulate** the user from it. Once inside, the VR universe can be coded to provide just about anything, ranging from a lightsaber battle with Darth Vader to a realistic (yet wholly invented) recreation of Earth. While VR has some business applications in product design, training, architecture, and retail, today the majority of VR applications are built around entertainment, especially gaming. Augmented reality, on the other hand, integrates the **simulated world** with the real one. In most applications the user relies on a smartphone or tablet screen to accomplish this, aiming the phone's camera at a point of interest and generating a **live-streaming video** of that scene on the screen. The screen is then **overlaid with** helpful information, which includes implementations such as repair instructions, navigation information, or diagnostic data. However, AR can also be used in entertainment applications. The mobile game Pokemon Go, in which players attempt to capture virtual creatures while moving around in the real world, is a classic example.

AR and VR are still in the infancy, and they have a

insulate 隔离

simulated world 模拟世界

live-streaming video 直播视频
overlay with 覆盖；充满

CHAPTER 7 Artificial Intelligence

long timeline of development ahead of them before they become true mainstream technologies. Some of the most frequently-cited technology and business challenges include:

- Limited mobile processing capability—Mobile handsets have limited processing power, but tethering a user to a desktop or server isn't realistic. Either mobile processing power will have to expand, or the work will have to be offloaded to the cloud.

- Limited mobile bandwidth—While cloud-based processing offers a compelling potential solution to the mobile processing bottleneck, mobile phone bandwidth is still too slow in most places to offer the necessary real-time video processing. This will likely change as mobile bandwidth improves.

- Complex development—Designing an AR or VR application is costly and complicated. Development tools will need to become more user-friendly to make these technologies accessible to programmers.

- VR hardware's inconvenience—Putting on a virtual reality headset and clearing a room often detract from the user experience. VR input devices, in the form of modified gaming controllers, can also often be unintuitive, with a **steep learning curve**.

steep learning curve 陡峭的学习曲线

- Building a business model—Outside of video gaming, many AR and VR applications remain in the early stages of development with unproven viability in the business world.

- Security and privacy issues—The **backlash** over the original Google Glass proved that the mainstream remains skeptical about the proliferation of cameras and their privacy implications. How

backlash 反对；抵制

149

are video feeds secured, and are copies stored somewhere?

Despite these challenges, however, significant progress is being made to expand both business and commercial use cases for AR and VR, and further drive them into the mainstream.

AR and VR have a decidedly bright future, and the years to come will bring many new capabilities and more widespread usage. Improvements in video quality, processing power, mobile bandwidth, and AR/VR hardware will drive more mainstream acceptance, and falling development costs and complexity will provide more options for creators to explore. Systems that track eye movement and facial expressions will slowly make clunky joysticks and other controllers obsolete.

While video gaming and entertainment will continue to drive this market, AR and VR will also see emerging practical applications. In the world of virtual reality, these include fully virtual surgery, in which surgeons perform their jobs only in a simulated environment and robotic systems do the actual work. In the world of AR, the ability to virtually travel anywhere is made possible by an emerging tech platform called Mirror World, which aims to replicate the physical universe on a 1:1 scale. Education will likely continue to shift to a virtual model on AR and VR platforms both in academia and in the corporate world. And finally, retailers will continue to rely on AR applications to upgrade virtual shopping applications, slowly rendering the need for physical storefronts obsolete.

(Source: Splunk Inc. website)

CHAPTER 7 Artificial Intelligence

Exercises

Task A **Decide whether the following statements are true (T) or false (F).**

1. Augmented reality augments your surroundings by replacing a real-life environment with a simulated one.
2. In virtual reality, the fabricated environment is usually designed to be much smaller than life.
3. Virtual reality replaces the real world with the virtual one, whereas augmented reality integrates the simulated world with the real one.
4. Due to limited mobile bandwidth, mobile phone bandwidth is still slow in most places to offer the necessary real-time video processing.
5. There is no need to worry about privacy issues of augmented reality and virtual reality, because the videos and copies have been coded.

Task B **Choose the word or phrase which is closest in meaning to the underlined part in each sentence.**

1. Virtual reality is a completely immersive experience that replaces a real-life environment with a <u>simulated</u> one.
   A. natural   B. imitative   C. false   D. ingenuine

2. In addition to entertainment <u>scenarios</u>, augmented reality is also increasingly being used by businesses, because of its ability to generate informational overlays that add useful, real-world scenarios.
   A. settings   B. senses   C. criteria   D. standards

3. AR and VR are still in the <u>infancy</u>, and they have a long timeline of development ahead of them before they become true mainstream technologies.
   A. development B. fragility   C. maturity   D. budding

4. VR hardware's inconvenience—Putting on a virtual reality headset and clearing a room often <u>detract from</u> the user experience.
   A. enhance   B. increase   C. impair   D. damage

5. The backlash over the original Google Glass proved that the mainstream remains <u>skeptical</u> about the proliferation of cameras and their privacy implications.
   A. cynical   B. unfriendly   C. credulous D. suspicious

151

Task C **Answer the following questions based on the text.**

1. What is the difference between AR and VR?

2. What are the technical challenges for AR and VR?

3. What are the business challenges for AR and VR?

4. Besides entertainment scenarios, are there any other emerging applications of AR and VR?

5. In education, which field will continue to change to a virtual model on AR and VR platforms?

Reading Tips 首/尾焦点与尾重原则

在语篇阅读过程中，为了快速抓住关键信息、提高阅读效率，读者必须谙熟英语语句的信息构建原则。在英语中，语句信息构建主要遵循两个原则：一个是倾向于把新信息或重要信息置于句子的起首或末尾，即首/尾焦点（head/end-focus）原则；另一个是倾向于把比较复杂的部分置于句子的末尾，即尾重（end-weight）原则。

1. 首/尾焦点原则

英语话语具有中心明了、重点突出的特点，其焦点意义在正常语序中总在句首或句尾出现，这和汉语中由于螺旋式思维而含蓄地把信息焦点放在语序的后部不同。

首焦点原则是指在复合句或信息内容冗杂的简单句中，信息焦点通常处于句子的起首位置。英语遵循直线型思维方式，习惯开门见山的表达方式，即把中心意思放在最前面，之后再层层展开或逐项分列。例如：

- **Other archaeologists study more recent cultures** by examining both their material remains and written documents, a practice known as historical archaeology.
- **The use of big data analytics in the healthcare industry has the potential to revolutionize patient care** by improving disease prevention, diagnosis, and treatment through personalized medicine and predictive analytics.
- **Work safety is one of the most important issues** that capture the greatest attention of people when the Chinese economy is growing rapidly.

上述三个例句都较好地体现了首焦点原则。其中，前两例属于信息内容较多的简单句，而后面一例是复合句。这些句子虽然都较长，但思路清晰、行文流畅，体现了英语母语者的思维方式。以最后一句为例：该句一上来就点出主题，即 Work safety is one of the most important issues，接着以 that 引导的定语从句对其重要性进行说明，最后以时间状语从句说明其背景。这种"事件—背景"的行文方式符合首焦点原则，可以较好地体现作者的交际意图，从而实现交际目的。

尾焦点原则是指在简单句中或当句子只有一个信息单位的情况下，新信息和重要信息倾向位于句子的末尾。这种词序的安排会在句尾形成一种高潮，使句子生动有力。例如：

- The new smartphone **has an improved camera, longer battery life, and faster processing speeds**.
- The autonomous vehicle **can detect obstacles, navigate complex environments, and safely transport passengers**.

虽然在含有多个信息单位的句子中也会出现信息焦点位于句末的情况，但一般而言，该原则主要适用于句法结构比较简单的句子中。需要注意的是，在正常的句法结构中，信息焦点的出现位置是相对固定的，但并不排除在被动句、强调句、特殊疑问句以及口语中为了特别强调而改变信息焦点位置的情形。

2. 尾重原则

尾重原则是影响英语句法结构的另一个重要原则，它是指把句子中最"笨重"或最复杂的成分放在句尾，形成"头小尾大"的结构。这有利于保持英语句子结构的平衡，避免头重脚轻。在句法结构比较复杂的句子中，首焦点和尾重原则往往相辅相成、相得益彰。英语中一般会避免较长的结构成分前置，而是通过分割、倒装等方法实现重量后移。例如：

- Regarding the automated driving legislation, **the U.S. introduced the Self Drive Act** to identify the federal role in ensuring the safety of automated vehicles and to encourage the testing and deployment of such vehicles.

在这个句子中，信息焦点是 the U.S. introduced the Self Drive Act，虽然目的状语很长，但在后置之后句子整体比较平衡，符合尾重原则。如果将状语提前，读者则需要阅读较多的内容才能看到真正的主语和焦点信息，难免抓不住句子主题，反而增加他们的认知负担。

再如，英语母语者习惯说"He explained to me that it was against law."，而不习惯说"He explained that it was against law to me."。他们之所以采用前一句结构，一个主要原因是 that 结构比介词短语用词多、结构要更复杂。前者听起来自然，因为它符合末尾加重的原则；后者听起来别扭，因为它不符合这一原则。

Section B Translation

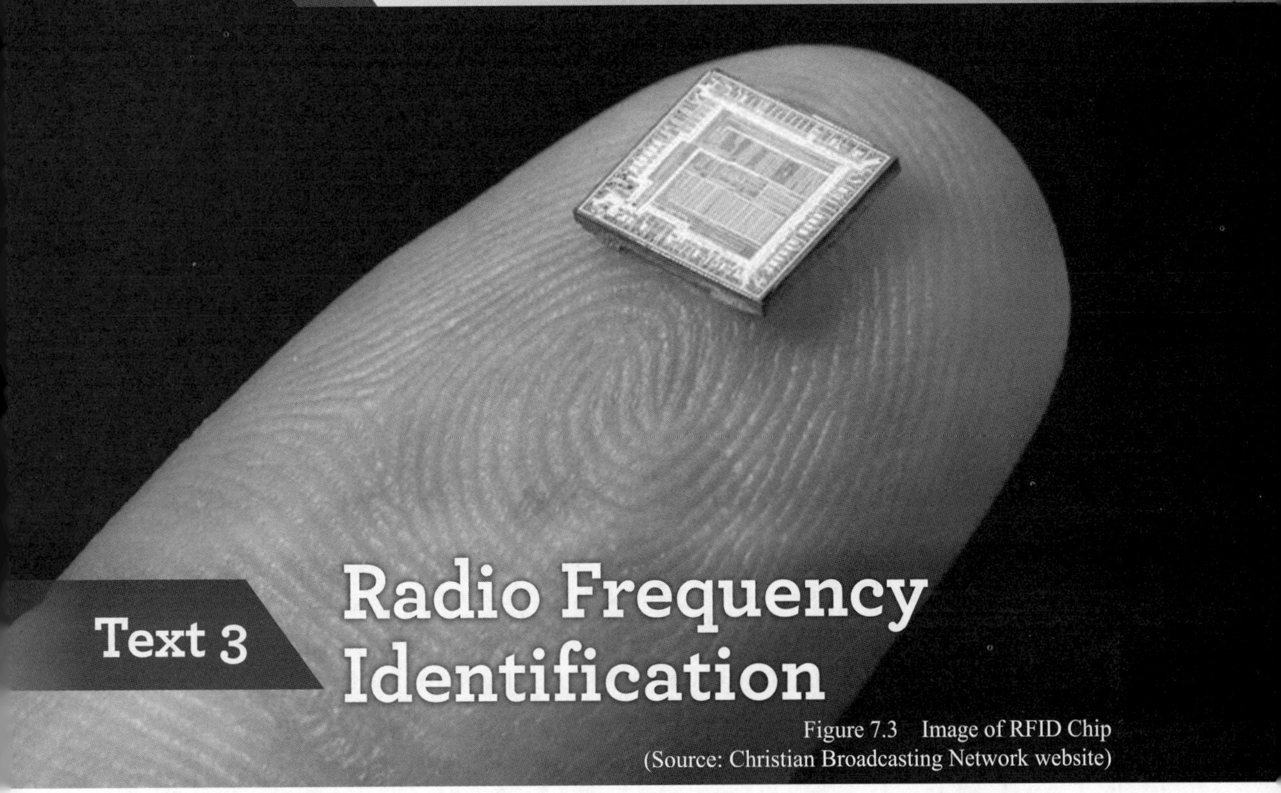

Text 3 Radio Frequency Identification

Figure 7.3 Image of RFID Chip
(Source: Christian Broadcasting Network website)

① Often the technologies that reshape daily life sneak up on us, until suddenly one day it's hard to imagine a world without them—instant messaging, for example, or microwave ovens. ② Other watershed technologies are visible a mile away, and when you contemplate their applications, the ultimate social impact looks enormous. ③ A good example is radio frequency identification (REID) chips.

④ An RFID chip is a tiny bit of silicon, smaller than a grain of rice, that carries information—anything from a retail price, to cooking instructions, to your complete medical records. ⑤ A larger piece of equipment called an RFID "reader" can, without direct contact, pull that information off the chip and in turn deliver it to any electronic device—a cash register, a video screen, a home appliance, even directly onto the Internet. ⑥ RFID is the technology used now to automate toll taking at bridges and tunnels; drivers are given a small plastic box with an RFID chip inside, allowing them to drive through the tollgates without stopping. ⑦ An RFID reader in the tollbooth senses the information on the chip and the toll is automatically deducted from the driver's account.

The first wide-scale application of RFID will be in retail. At a major industry conference next week, Walmart is expected to urge its suppliers to adopt RFID—the same way that, 20 years ago, the giant retailer jump-started the use of bar codes. And some manufacturers are already on board. Gillette, for example, recently placed an order for half a billion RFID chips that they will begin to use to track razors.

Ultimately, a reader on every retail shelf will be able to automatically sense when the store is low on inventory and automatically place an order to restock. RFID should also permit more accurate tracking of merchandise within the store drastically reducing the theft or other losses generically called shrinkage in the retail business. And RFID will ultimately allow consumers to simply walk past the cash register with their purchases; the register will read the RFID chips and automatically deduct the purchase from their account. Where was RFID when Winona Ryder needed it?

Inventory and checkout counters, however, are only the start of possible RFID applications. Japanese bookstores, for example, plan to use RFID to track how customers use books in the store: How many times and how long is each book taken off the shelf to read, before someone actually buys it? The European Union is considering placing a tiny RFID chip in every paper Euro note providing both counterfeiting protection and the ability to give each bill a unique serial number. An American company, VeriChip, is developing an RFID chip implant that will permanently store your medical records under your skin, so any hospital equipped with a reader can know all your pertinent health information even if you are unconscious. A simpler version of this subcutaneous chip is already implanted to help identify pets.

(Source: Cryptogon website)

Exercises

Task A **Review the original translation of the underlined sentences in the source text and make any necessary revisions. Then learn how to improve your revisions from the analysis and modification of the translation provided.**

这篇短文介绍了无线射频技术及其在日常生活中的应用。译文评析如下：

> 原文①： Often the technologies that reshape daily life sneak up on us, until suddenly one day it's hard to imagine a world without them—instant messaging, for example, or microwave ovens.

CHAPTER **7** Artificial Intelligence

> 初译①：那些改变我们日常生活的技术往往在不知不觉中靠近我们，如果突然有一天没有它们（例如即时通信和微波炉），我们很难想象世界将是什么样。

学生评改：_____

> 评析：初译①基本上传递了原文的信息，但是准确性有待提高。具体而言，sneak up on 和 instant messaging 的翻译都存在这一问题。根据词典释义，sneak up on 确实有"慢慢接近"的意思，但如果按此直译（"不知不觉中靠近我们"），则会让读者认为这些技术尚未进入人们的生活，而实际情况是它们已经进入人们的日常生活，只是人们没有察觉到。因而，此处应适当地进行引申翻译。另外，将 instant messaging 翻译成"即时通信"也不准确，属于扩大词义范围的做法。根据词典释义——"An instant message is a written message that is sent from one computer to another."——可知，它主要是指书面形式的短消息。
>
> 改译：那些彻底改变日常生活的技术往往在不知不觉中进入我们的生活，很难想象，如果有一天它们（比如短信息、微波炉）突然从我们的生活中消失，世界将会变成什么样。

> 原文②③：Other watershed technologies are visible a mile away, and when you contemplate their applications, the ultimate social impact looks enormous. A good example is radio frequency identification (RFID) chips.
>
> 初译②③：不久我们还将看到其他重要技术的出现，我们可以预见，这些技术的应用将引起巨大的社会效应。无线射频识别（简称 RFID）芯片就是一个很好的例子。

学生评改：_____
_____
_____

评析：原文②的翻译难点在于时态问题。初译②采用了多个表示将来时态的用词，如"不久""将""预见"等，但是原文中并没有明显的表示将来时态的词汇。之所以会做出这样的判断，主要是因为对 visible a mile away（一英里外可见）这个短语的理解出现偏差。这个隐喻想要表达的是很多技术离人们的生活并不遥远，指的是空间层面而非时间概念。因为从下文可以发现，原文作者举的例子（"无线射频识别芯片"）其实已经在日常生活中得到广泛的应用，而非未来的一项技术。因此，整个译文的时态应该由将来时转变为一般现在时。初译③基本上传递了原文信息。

改译：还有一些重要技术离我们的生活并不遥远，深入思考你就会发现这些技术应用对社会的影响极其深远。无线射频识别（简称RFID）芯片就是一个典型的例子。

原文④：An RFID chip is a tiny bit of silicon, smaller than a grain of rice, that carries information—anything from a retail price, to cooking instructions, to your complete medical records.

初译④：芯片是比米粒还小的硅片，存有各种信息——从零售价格、烹饪指南，到你的全部病历，一应俱全。

学生评改：_____

_____

评析：原文④是对RFID芯片的整体介绍，初译基本上传递了原文信息，但在准确度和流利性方面还有待进一步完善。首先，原句是一个含有定语从句和插入语（smaller than a grain of rice）的复合句，二者之间存在转折关系，因此可以通过增译逻辑连接词"虽然……但是"来提升译文的连贯性。而英文破折号之后的内容是通过列举进行的补充说明。其中，"零售价格"的表述不准确，建议修改为"商品销售价格"；而 your complete medical records 直译为"你的全部病历"过于口语化，建议修改为"个人病历记录"。为了提升译文效果，也可以全部采取四字短语，如"商品价格、烹饪指南、病历记录"。

改译：RFID芯片虽然是比米粒还小的硅片，但可以存储各种信息，如商品销售价格、烹饪指南、个人病历记录等。

CHAPTER **7** Artificial Intelligence

原文⑤：A larger piece of equipment called an RFID "reader" can, without direct contact, pull that information off the chip and in turn deliver it to any electronic device—a cash register, a video screen, a home appliance, even directly onto the Internet.

初译⑤：还有一种较大的设备，称作 RFID "阅读器"，它不必与 RFID 芯片直接连接就可以从芯片中下载信息，并将其输入任何电子设备（如收款机、视频屏幕、家用电器），甚至直接进入互联网。

学生评改：_____

评析：初译⑤的整体质量较好，仅在个别词汇、短语的翻译上不够准确。例如，contact 应直接翻译成"接触"，而不是"连接"，因为 RFID "阅读器"在实际应用时主要通过物理空间的接近来实现二者之间的联系或连接。而 pull that information off the chip 翻译成"下载信息"不如"读取信息"更为专业和准确，因为"阅读器"的主要功能是"读取"而非"下载"。括号中列举的电子设备和后文的互联网是并列关系，可以放在括号之外，并不影响阅读效果。另外，一些表述不够准确和规范，如"视频屏幕""进入互联网"等都应当进行修改。

改译：还有一种较大的设备，称作 RFID "阅读器"，它不必与 RFID 芯片直接接触就可以从芯片中读取信息，并将信息输入任何电子设备，如收银机、显示屏、家用电器，甚至可以直接上传到互联网。

原文⑥⑦：RFID is the technology used now to automate toll taking at bridges and tunnels; drivers are given a small plastic box with an RFID chip inside, allowing them to drive through the tollgates without stopping. An RFID reader in the tollbooth senses the information on the chip and the toll is automatically deducted from the driver's account.

初译⑥⑦：目前，RFID 技术已用于桥梁与隧道的自动收款业务，方法是发给司机一个装有 RFID 芯片的小塑料盒子，这样他就可以通过收费关卡而无需停车，收款亭中的 RFID 阅读器会感知芯片上的信息，于是过路费就会自动从司机的账户中扣除。

学生评改：_____

_____

_____

_____

> **评析**：原文⑥和⑦主要介绍了 RFID 技术在自动收款业务中的应用。初译通顺性欠佳，主要问题在于表达过于啰唆、冗余。比如，"方法是发给司机一个装有 RFID 芯片的小塑料盒子"完全可以简化为"司机只需在车内安装一个带有 RFID 芯片的小塑料盒"；"这样他就可以"可以简化为"就可以"。另外，tollbooth 翻译为"收款亭"不够地道，应改为"收费站"。
>
> **改译**：目前，RFID 技术已应用于桥梁和隧道的自动收款业务，司机只需在车内安装一个带有 RFID 芯片的小塑料盒就可以直接通过收费站而不必停车。收费站中的 RFID 阅读器会读取芯片上的信息，之后过路费会从司机的账户中自动扣除。

Task B Translate the following text into Chinese.

Our brains have a remarkable ability to assimilate motor skills that allow us to perform a host of tasks almost automatically—driving a car, riding a bicycle, typing on a keyboard, etc. Now add another to the list: operating a computer using only thoughts.

Researchers at the University of California, Berkeley, have demonstrated how rhesus monkeys with electrodes implanted in their brains used their thoughts to control a computer cursor. Once the animals had mastered the task, they could repeat it proficiently day after day. The ability to repeat such feats is unprecedented in the field of neuroprosthetics. It reflects a major finding by scientists: A monkey's brain is able to develop a motor memory for controlling a virtual device in a manner similar to the way it creates such a memory for the animal's body.

The new study, which should apply to humans, provides hope that physically disabled people may one day be able to operate advanced prosthetics in a natural, effortless way. Previous research in brain-machine interfaces, or BMIs, had already shown that monkeys and humans could use thought to

CHAPTER 7 Artificial Intelligence

control robots and computers in real time. But subjects weren't able to retain the skills from one session to another, and the BMI system had to be recalibrated every session. In this new study, as long as monkeys do, monkeys won't forget.

Translation Tips 长难句的翻译方法

科技语篇描写的是科学原理、规律、概念以及各事物之间错综复杂的关系，给出的定义、定律、定理、工艺过程等都必须严谨、准确，因此不可避免地会使用一些结构比较复杂的长句。在这些长句中，常常是一个主句带若干个从句，从句带短语、短语带从句、从句套从句，它们互相依附、互相制约，一环扣一环，可谓错综复杂、盘根错节。在遇到科技英语长难句时，译者需要以句法和逻辑为导向，抓住复杂句的核心，通过辨清主谓来确定句子的基本格局，从而才能把握全句的结构。朱俊松（2002）提出英语长句的分析应该遵循以下四个步骤：

第一步，先把长难句分解为若干小句。通过句法分析，抓住句子的主干，将长难句划分为若干小句。

第二步，逐一分析小句，厘清语法成分。将小句简化为"主+谓+宾"或"主+系+表"结构，暂时将句子的其他成分（各种短语与附加成分）搁置一边，以便抓住句子的主要矛盾。

第三步，研究各小句之间的逻辑关系。将句子进行复原，再次进行句法结构分析，判断小句之间的逻辑关系，做到泾渭分明、脉络清楚。

第四步，全句翻译。

举例说明：

原文：The scope of the book is such that it should provide a solid foundation for those who intend to select optics as a career and at the same time, it should furnish an adequate knowledge of the subject in a comprehensible form for those who intend to specialize in other branches of physics or engineering.

第一步，把复合句分解为若干简单句。

① The scope of the book is such

② that it should provide a solid foundation for those

③ who intend to select optics as a career

④ and at the same time, it should furnish an adequate knowledge of the subject in a comprehensible form for those

⑤ who intend to specialize in other branches of physics or engineering

第二步，分析各简单句中词与词之间的关系。

① 中 The scope 是主语，of the book 是定语，is such 是谓语。

② 中 that 是引导词，it 是主语，should provide 是谓语，a solid foundation 是宾语，for those 是状语。

③ 中 who 是主语，intend 是谓语，to select optics as a career 是宾语。

CHAPTER 7　Artificial Intelligence

④ 中 and 是连词，at the same time 是状语，it 是主语，should furnish 是谓语，an adequate knowledge 是宾语，of the subject 是定语，in a comprehensible form for those 是状语。

⑤ 中 who 是主语，intend 是谓语，to specialize 是宾语，in other branches 是状语，of physics or engineering 是定语。

第三步，分析句与句之间的关系。

这是并列主从复合句：①是主句；②是结果状语从句；③是定语从句，修饰②中的 those；④是结果状语从句，与②构成并列复合句；⑤是定语从句，修饰④中的 those（见图 7.1）。

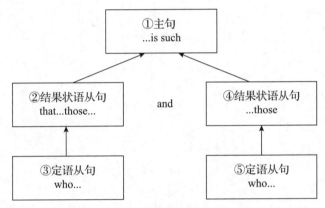

图 7.1　各小句之间的关系

第四步，全句翻译。

译文：本书可以为那些打算选择光学专业的读者提供牢固的基础知识，同时可以为物理学或工程学等其他专业的读者提供易于理解的光学知识。

CHAPTER 8
Energy and Ecology

Introduction

We are all aware that shortages of natural resources can impact ecosystems and cause the deterioration of the natural environment. Therefore, we have been focusing on approaches that integrate considerations of energy, ecology, and environment, and endeavoring to utilize their cross-disciplinary integration to function as a needed counterbalance to the dominant economic approach. In this chapter, Text 1 is a passage for fast reading, dealing with the future of alternative energy sources; Text 2 is a passage for intensive reading, introducing low-carbon economy; and Text 3 is a passage for translation, discussing climate change and global warming. The learning objective of this chapter is to familiarize the learners with the Theme-Rheme structure of EST and cohesion and coherence in passage translation of EST.

Lead-in Questions

1. Do you think it is necessary to promote multidisciplinary studies to set up systems for tackling complex energy and environmental problems?
2. What do you know about the following topics: energy economics, life cycle assessment, carbon capture, storage, and sequestration, and sustainable energy production and consumption?

Section A Fast and Intensive Reading

Text 1

Why Are Alternative Energy Sources the Future?

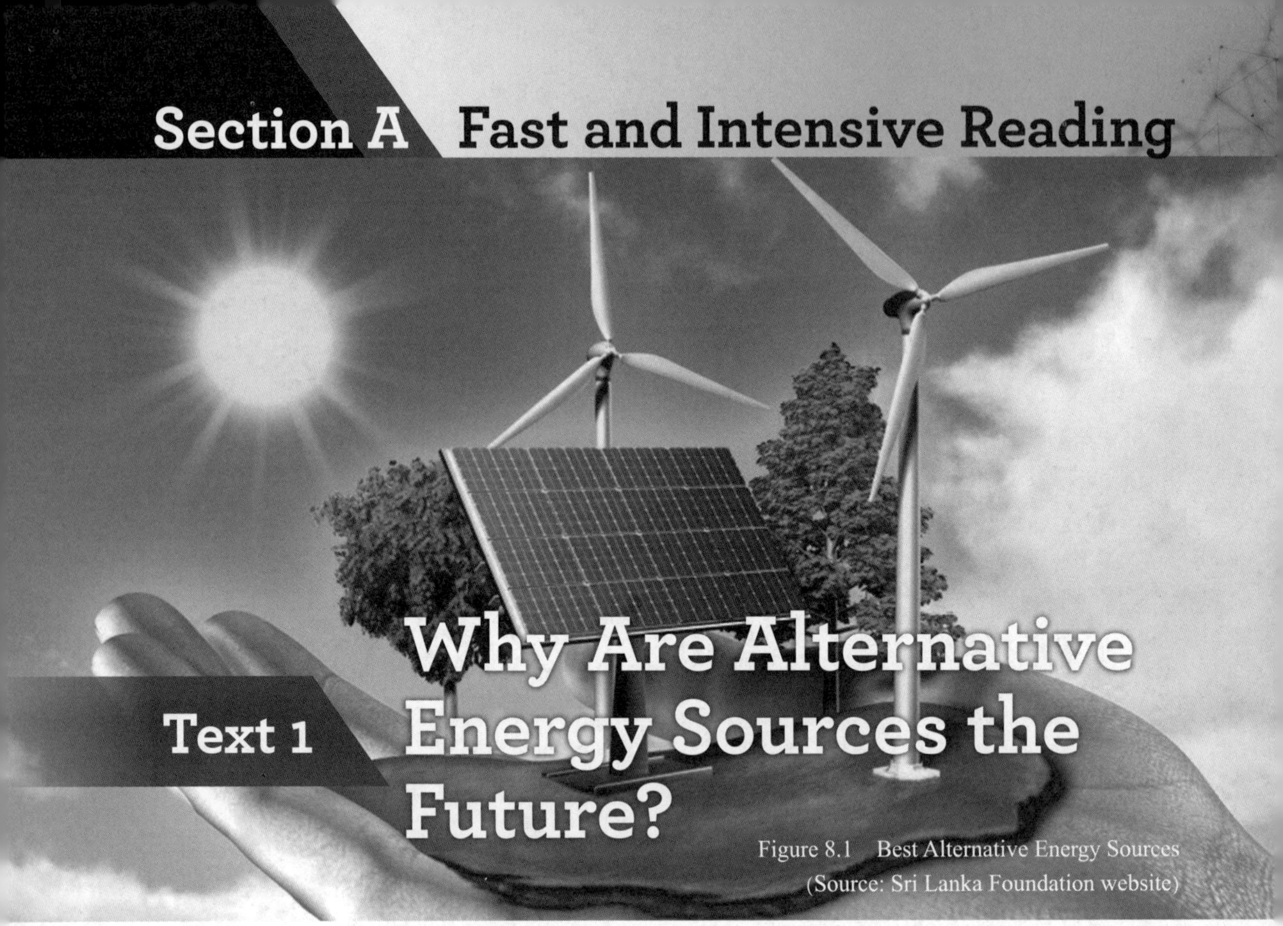

Figure 8.1 Best Alternative Energy Sources
(Source: Sri Lanka Foundation website)

A   Our current level of dependence on fossil fuels puts us on track for a rapid depletion of these finite materials. Meaning, if we're not careful, we will run out of our precious, non-renewable resources. That means no more oil, natural gas, and even coal. Burning fossil fuels in power plants is also hard on the environment. We're talking about everything from ocean and air pollution to the destruction of entire ecosystems.

B   The good news is that we're now able to reduce our dependence on fossil fuels like oil, coal, and natural gas, thanks to the growth of alternative energy sources. This article will discuss what alternative energy is and why it's so important that we transition from our dependence on fossil fuels to alternative energy sources. We'll also take a look at the difference between alternative and renewable energy sources, along with what sources of energy we're using today to meet our energy needs.

C   Fossil fuels (oil, coal, and natural gas) are our most traditional source for power generation. Therefore, the energy that's produced from any source other than fossil fuels is alternative energy. In other words, alternative energy is any amount of energy derived from non-fossil fuel sources. Generally speaking, using alternative energy has a low environmental impact.

D   We now know that alternative energy sources are any source we use to

CHAPTER 8 Energy and Ecology

supplement or even replace traditional energy sources used for power generation. You could almost say the same thing about renewable energy sources. But there is one subtle difference between the two. All renewable energy sources fall under the category of alternative energy sources, but it doesn't work the other way around. That's because renewable energy sources are derived from naturally replenished sources or processes of Earth, such as the Sun, wind, and water. We refer to these resources as renewable or sustainable (as in sustainable energy) since, unlike fossil fuels, this naturally occurring continual renewal makes them inexhaustible. However, it's possible for there to be alternative energy sources that are exhaustible, and therefore not renewable. That's the difference. So what alternative energy source is exhaustible?

E   The equipment necessary to harness energy from alternative sources used to be so expensive that it wasn't practical for consumer use. However, thanks to increased demand, more experienced energy developers, competitive supply chains, improved renewable technologies, and enhanced energy efficiency capabilities, that's no longer the case. In fact, renewable power has now become increasingly cheaper than fossil fuels for electricity generation. Let's look at a few of the best alternative energy sources we use today.

F   Onshore wind power and solar photovoltaics, respectively, are currently the most affordable options when it comes to energy production. Using these two natural resources over coal could save as much as $23 billion in yearly power system expenses. It could also lower annual carbon dioxide emissions by 1.8 gigatons. Bioenergy, geothermal energy, hydroelectric power, and nuclear energy are also making their way into the financially competitive spotlight, depending significantly on location.

G   When it comes to energy efficiency, the leader of the renewable energy pack is wind energy. Behind wind come geothermal energy, hydropower, nuclear energy, and then solar power.

H   Out of all the known energy sources, nuclear energy has the highest capacity factor by far. Nuclear power plants are able to produce maximum power over 93% of the time on an annual basis. Next in line comes geothermal, followed by natural gas. Natural gas is considered the cleanest burning and most reliable fossil fuel, but it still isn't a clean energy resource. However, there is an alternative called renewable natural gas (RNG). RNG also goes by the name of biomethane and is produced from livestock, landfill waste, and other organic materials through anaerobic digestion. While it's not a fossil fuel, RNG is completely identical to conventional natural gas in chemical make-up, allowing

them to use the same distribution system.

I As it turns out, wind energy, which uses turbines to harness its power from the wind, is one of the cleanest and most sustainable forms of electricity generation. It's able to produce energy without generating any pollutants or global warming emissions. Plus, the land and animal impact of wind turbines is minimal.

J What are the nine most commonly used alternative energy sources? Here's a quick-reference list of some of the most common sustainable energy resources that we use today: wind energy, solar energy, hydroelectric energy, geothermal energy, bioenergy, nuclear energy, hydrogen energy, tidal energy, and wave energy.

K As alternative energy technologies continue to improve, the cost simultaneously falls. Solar and wind power have unlocked the potential to generate an energy reserve plentiful enough to meet the world's demand. When you look at how affordable, effective, and economically friendly these powerhouses are, you begin to see how we could displace fossil fuels within the next 30 years. Most consumers agree that the benefits of using alternative energy sources far outweigh any drawbacks. Not to mention, improved technology is continually emerging to address and eliminate the disadvantages of various renewable resources.

L You now understand the importance of making the switch to alternative energy sources and why it's so vital to a healthy future, but how can you go about making this necessary change? You may like to choose a new electricity plan or natural gas plan as part of your energy conservation efforts. Inquire about green energy products and plan options to get started on your new sustainable lifestyle.

(Source: Just Energy website)

bioenergy: a type of energy produced by using organic substances that can be replaced naturally, such as wood or vegetable oil   生物质能；生物能源

geothermal energy: a type of energy derived from the heat in the interior of the Earth   地热能

onshore wind power: a power that's generated by wind turbines located on land driven by the natural movement of the air   陆上风力发电（相对于海上风力发电 [offshore wind power]）

solar photovoltaics: more commonly known as solar panels that generate power using devices that absorb energy from sunlight and convert it into electrical energy through semiconducting materials 光电子能；太阳光电；太阳能光伏

Exercises

Task A **Identify the paragraph from which each of the following statements is derived. You may choose a paragraph more than once. Each paragraph in the above text is marked with a letter.**

1. Wind energy is least damaging to the environment.
2. Solar photovoltaics is one of the two most affordable choices for energy production.
3. There is one subtle difference between renewable and alternative energy sources.
4. Alternative energy can effectively replace fossil fuels in the future.
5. Fossil fuel materials are limited and burning fossil fuels is bad for the environment.
6. Renewable power has become affordable owing to the increased demand.
7. Renewable natural gas is a reliable and clean energy source.
8. Alternative energy is any amount of energy other than oil, coal, and natural gas.
9. Wind energy is the most efficient alternative energy source.
10. We are less dependent on fossil fuels because we transition to alternative energy sources.

Task B **Work in groups to discuss the following topic and share your opinions with the class.**

Transition from Fossil Fuels to Alternative Energy

　　The global warming crisis is becoming increasingly urgent, and it is imperative that we take action to address it. One of the key ways we can help mitigate the effects of climate change is by shifting our reliance from fossil fuels to renewable and alternative energy sources. These include wind, solar, geothermal, and hydroelectric power, among others. In your opinion, what can individuals and communities do to support this transition?

Figure 8.2 Low-carbon Economy
(Source: Cummins Inc. website)

Text 2

Moving to a Competitive Low-carbon Economy

The **Low-carbon Roadmap** sets out cost-efficient pathways for key economic sectors for achieving an overall 80% reduction in the EU's emissions by 2050 (compared to 1990). This would be accomplished solely through **reduction measures** within the EU and does not include the possible use of international credits to offset emissions.

Extensive economic modeling undertaken to prepare the Roadmap shows that domestic emission cuts of the order of 40% and 60% below 1990 levels could be achieved in a cost-effective way by 2030 and 2040, respectively. Current policies are projected to reduce emissions domestically by 30% in 2030 and 40% in 2050.

By 2009, the EU reduced **greenhouse gas** emissions by around 16% compared to 1990 levels, whereas the economy grew by 40% over the same period. For 2020, member states have committed to reducing emissions by 20%, to increasing the share of **renewables** in the EU's energy mix to 20%, and to achieving a 20% energy efficiency improvement. With full implementation of current policies, the EU is on track to achieve a 20% domestic reduction in 2020 below 1990 levels. However,

Low-carbon Roadmap
低碳路线图

reduction measure 减排措施

greenhouse gas 温室气体

renewables 可再生能源

CHAPTER 8 Energy and Ecology

with current policies, only half of the 20% energy efficiency target would be met by 2020.

The **Energy Efficiency Plan** (EEP) presented at the same time as the Roadmap for moving to a low-carbon economy in 2050, sets out the necessary measures to achieve this energy efficiency target. Among other things, the EEP proposes binding targets for the **refurbishment rate** of public buildings, energy efficiency requirements for industrial equipment, energy audits, improving the efficiency of power and heat generation, and the roll-out of **smart power grids**.

If the EU delivers on its current policies, including its commitment to reach 20% renewables and achieve 20% energy efficiency by 2020, this would enable the EU to outperform the current 20% emission reduction target and achieve a 25% reduction by 2020. In international climate negotiations, the EU's conditional offer to reduce emissions by 30% over the next decade if other major economies make similar efforts remains very much on the table, but these conditions have not been met yet.

The modeling and analyses which the Roadmap builds on take into account global trends such as population growth, evolution of oil prices, technological developments, and different levels of global climate action. The impacts on Europe's competitive sectors were projected to assess the risk of stepping up climate action without our main competitors doing so as well.

Making our economies energy-efficient and climate-friendly would lead to a massive shift from fuel expenses to investment expenditure. The investments will add value to and increase output from our domestic economy, while fuel expenses largely flow out of the EU.

Over the next 40 years, additional annual investment equivalent to 1.5% of the EU's GDP, or around €270

Energy Efficiency Plan
能源效率计划

refurbishment rate 翻修率

smart power grid 智能电网

billion, would be needed on top of current annual investment equivalent to 19% of GDP. The increase would simply bring back the EU's overall investment expenditure to the level before the economic crisis. In comparison, in 2009 emerging economies like China (48%), India (35%), and Korea (26%) allocated much larger shares of GDP to investments.

Energy consumption will go down by almost 30%, thanks to improved energy efficiency, from 1,800 million tons of oil equivalent (**Mtoe**) in 2005, to 1,650 Mtoe in 2030 and 1,300–1,350 Mtoe in 2050.

Mtoe 百万吨石油当量

More domestic energy sources will be used, in particular wind, solar, biomass, and water. This will improve the EU's security of energy supply and make our economies less vulnerable to oil price shocks. By 2050, fossil fuel imports will be more than halved compared to today; whereas without action, these imports are projected to double. Over the whole 40-year period, average fuel costs will fall by between €175 billion and €320 billion a year.

Air pollution levels would on average be more than 65% lower in 2030 than in 2005. This would reduce healthcare and mortality costs drastically, by €7–€17 billion a year by 2030 and by €17–€38 billion a year by 2050. In addition, savings on air pollution control measures could amount to close to €50 billion a year by 2050.

Delaying climate action would require additional investment expenditure of around €100 billion per year between 2030 and 2050, but would not reduce investment needs before 2030 by a comparable amount. Also, fuel savings would be lower over time.

Renewable energy has a strong track record in job creation. In just five years, the renewable industry has increased its workforce from 230,000 to 550,000. A 25% reduction in the EU's greenhouse gas emissions could create 1.5 million additional jobs by the end of this decade if governments use revenues from auctioning of **CO_2 emissions** and carbon taxes to reduce labor costs.

CO_2 emission 二氧化碳排放

In the longer term, the creation and preservation of jobs will depend on the EU's ability to lead in the development of new low-carbon technologies through increased education, training, R&D, and innovation, as well as maintaining favorable economic framework conditions for investments. Changing the energy system, transport, and the housing sector will increase the demand for new skills and competences. Sectors that will profit most from **"decarbonizing"** the economy are construction, power, transport, and renewable energy.

decarbonize 脱碳

The recovery of construction sector, which was particularly hard hit by the economic crisis, could get a significant boost through a major effort to accelerate the renovation and building of energy-efficient houses. Investments in residential and commercial buildings are projected to increase by €20 billion a year over the coming decade, raising annual investment to €70 billion. The additional investment could create or maintain 150,000–500,000 direct construction jobs a year.

Under decarbonization, scenarios investments in smart grids and clean power plants are also projected to increase by more €30 billion annually by 2030. A recent study by the European Commission has estimated that an additional €50 billion investment in this sector would add 400,000 direct and indirect jobs.

(Source: The European Commission website)

Exercises

Task A Decide whether the following statements are true (T) or false (F).

1. The Low-carbon Roadmap put forward by the EU will be accomplished by reduction measures and the use of international credits to offset emissions.

2. With full implementation of current policies, the EU has achieved a 20% domestic reduction in 2020 below 1990 levels.

3. Other major economies have promised to make similar efforts as those of the EU in international climate negotiations.

4. It is believed that making economies energy-efficient would decrease fuel expenses and increase investment expenditure.

5. The construction sector can recover from the economic crisis by a boost in the renovation and building of energy-efficient houses.

Task B Choose the word or phrase which is closest in meaning to the underlined part in each sentence.

1. The Low-carbon Roadmap <u>sets out</u> cost-efficient pathways for key economic sectors for achieving an overall 80% reduction in the EU's emissions by 2050 (compared to 1990).

    A. argues　　　B. expects　　　C. presents　　　D. leads

2. The impacts on Europe's competitive sectors were projected to <u>assess</u> the risk of stepping up climate action without our main competitors doing so as well.

    A. evaluate　　　B. count　　　C. reduce　　　D. eradicate

3. By 2050, fossil fuel imports will be more than halved compared to today; whereas without action, these imports are <u>projected</u> to double.

    A. believed　　　B. estimated　　　C. promised　　　D. doomed

4. This would reduce healthcare and <u>mortality</u> costs drastically, by €7–€17 billion a year by 2030 and by €17–€38 billion a year by 2050.

    A. caring　　　B. nursing　　　C. illness　　　D. death

5. The recovery of construction sector, which was particularly hard hit by the economic crisis, could get a significant boost through a major effort to accelerate the <u>renovation</u> and building of energy-efficient houses.

    A. maintenance　　B. refurbishment　　C. construction　　D. removement

CHAPTER 8 Energy and Ecology

Task C **Answer the following questions based on the text.**

1. According to the Energy Efficiency Plan, what measures will be taken to achieve the energy efficiency target?
2. What is the EU's conditional offer in international climate negotiations?
3. What are the possible benefits that the low-carbon economy may bring to the EU?
4. What is the amount of investment required to return the EU's overall investment expenditure to the pre-crisis level?
5. By 2050, how much can we save on air pollution control measures every year?

Reading Tips 科技语篇的主述位推进模式

语篇信息不是杂乱无章地组织在一起的，而是以清晰和结构化的方式进行组织或构建的，呈现出特定的信息推进模式。把握语篇信息推进模式可以帮助读者了解信息的布局和指向，更好地领会作者想要表达的目的和主要信息，从而提高阅读速度。主述位结构（Theme-Rheme structure）对于句子及篇章的构建起着重要作用，它既适用于分析句子内部的信息分布，也适用于通过主述位推进模式（Theme-Rheme progression）分析来把握语篇的整体脉络。识别主述位结构是阅读训练的一种有效方法，能够对语篇布局有更加深入和准确的理解。

1. 主述位结构

在主述位结构中，主位既是信息的出发点、对象或基础，又是信息的附着点，是叙述内容的起点；述位既是信息的主体，又是对这一出发点的陈述、描述和说明，是叙述的核心内容。从句子结构来看，主位通常位于句子的开头，而述位是除主位以外的其他句子成分。

简单句中的主述位结构如下所示：

- The Earth（主位）revolves around the Sun（述位）.
- In space exploration（主位） China achieved a new milestone（述位）.
- There is a major breakthrough（主位）in cancer research（述位）.
- What gene（主位）is most likely to explain these clinical findings（述位）?
- The human body（主位）is made up of trillions of cells, isn't it（述位）?
- Is human brain（主位）the most complex organ in the body（述位）?

复合句中的主述位结构如下所示：

- It is quite obvious（主位）that the periodic table contains all known elements（述位）.
- We know that DNA（主位）carries genetic information and determines an organism's traits（述位）.
- If it doesn't take into account quantum mechanics（主位），why are we using this model（述位）?
- What we need to advance now in this field（主位）is gene editing technology（述位）.

在上面的例子中，主位不一定是主语本身，它可以是单词、词组或小句。通常情况下，一个句子的已知信息和主位是重合的，述位部分表示新的未知信息。"主位—已知信息"与"述位—未知信息"是最常见的主位结构与信息结构的对应关系。

CHAPTER 8 Energy and Ecology

2. 主述位推进模式

主述位结构是构成一个语篇的基本框架和信息分布导图,通过对语篇主述位结构的分析,读者可以较准确地掌握作者的整体思路及中心议题,从而实现对语篇的有效理解。主位—述位的排列组合主要是以主述位推进模式展开的,英语主述位推进模式主要有以下四种类型,如图8.1所示:

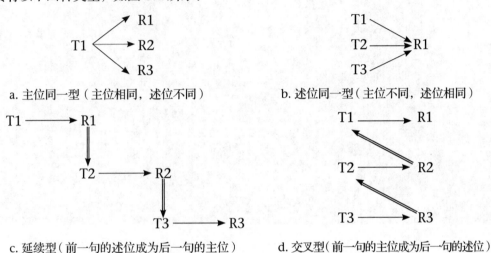

注:T 表示主位 Theme;R 表示述位 Rheme;数字表示小句序号

图 8.1　英语主述位推进模式的四种类型

在上述四种模式中,主述位不断将新信息向前扩展和推进,话语的推动和展开得以实现,语篇的衔接和连贯才得以完成。科技语篇一般是以主位同一型为主,以段落主题句的关键词为话语的出发点,线索清晰,分析层层推进。根据段落的长短不同,有时会在较长的段落里灵活地使用其他主述位推进模式。总而言之,主述位推进模式是语篇内主述位之间的相互联系、照应、衔接和过渡,对主述位推进模式的分析将有助于读者快速地把握整篇文章的布局谋篇和逻辑结构。

Section B Translation

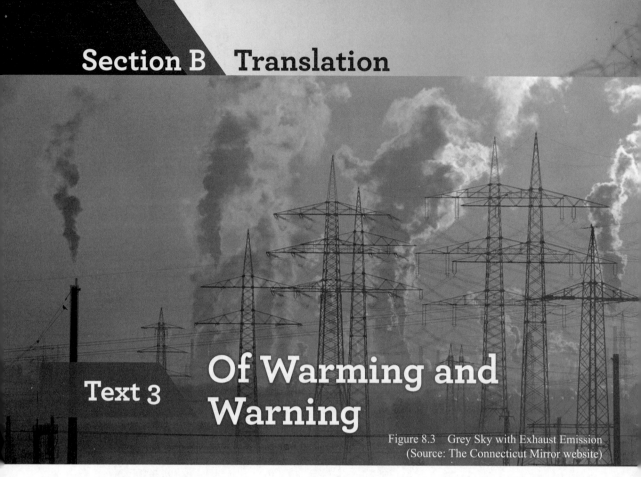

Text 3 Of Warming and Warning

Figure 8.3 Grey Sky with Exhaust Emission
(Source: The Connecticut Mirror website)

① "Science has spoken," said Ban Ki-moon, the UN's Secretary-General, "time is not on our side. Leaders must act." ② He was reacting to the latest assessment of the state of the global climate by the Intergovernmental Panel on Climate Change (IPCC), a group of scientists who advise governments.

③ Rajendra Pachauri, the IPCC's chairman, agreed. ④ "We have little time before the window of opportunity to stay within 2°C of warming closes," he said. (Governments have promised not to let global temperatures rise by more than that amount compared with pre-industrial levels.) ⑤ Bill McKibben, an American climate campaigner, went for broke, calling the report "just short of announcing that climate change will produce a zombie apocalypse, plus random beheadings, plus Ebola".

⑥ The assessment, it should be said, is sobering. ⑦ But it does not justify alarmism.

The IPCC's overview is its fifth since 1990. Things have moved on since the previous one, in 2007. Scientists have become ever more certain that human activity is to blame for climate change: about 95% certain, in fact (the first report said climate change was as likely as not a product of natural variation). The report spells out the evidence that the climate is indeed changing. Average land

CHAPTER 8 Energy and Ecology

and sea-surface temperatures rose by 0.85℃ in 1880–2012; sea levels rose by 3.2 mm a year in 1993–2010, twice as fast as in 1901–2010; the acidity of the ocean's surface has risen by 26% since the start of the Industrial Revolution.

At the moment, the impact of all this change can be seen mostly on natural systems. Arctic sea ice, for example, is shrinking by around 4% a decade, and the Greenland and Antarctic ice sheets are losing mass. Marine species are shifting their ranges, heading towards the poles to find cooler waters.

In contrast, the impact on human welfare has so far been modest. The report calls the effect on health "relatively small [and] not well-quantified". It expresses low confidence in the idea that the frequency and sizes of floods have been affected by climate change—though that is partly because the records are poor. True, it says, climate change in the form of heat and drought may have reduced yields of maize and wheat. But the effect on rice and soybeans, the world's other staple crops, has not been so bad. Although humans are damaging the climate, it is less clear that climate change is so far damaging humans that much.

If climate change is an emergency, then it is not of the kind that can be quickly reversed. Rather, the report says, actions taken now will have little impact for decades, mainly because the climate has exceptionally long response times. The Earth now has what is known in the parlance as a stock problem, not a flow problem. The flow of greenhouse gases into the atmosphere can be adjusted, but the stock of them already accumulated means that the expected rise in surface temperatures between 2016 and 2035 is roughly the same in a range of projections for how things might now go.

Claims that the report is all doom and gloom therefore refer to the middle of the century and later. Then, the IPCC suggests, there could be "severe, pervasive, and irreversible impacts". Inevitably, though, forecasts that far ahead come with significant qualifications. The size of the population, for example, makes a big difference to carbon emissions and climate change. But the difference between the UN's highest and lowest projections for 2050 is 2.5 billion people. The climate models themselves are a work in constant progress. Taken in sum, this latest assessment is a stern warning, but it is not yet a promise of disaster.

Correction: An earlier version of this article suggested that the "severe, pervasive, and irreversible impacts" mentioned by the IPCC would only occur in its worst-case projections. In fact, the report makes no such qualification. Sorry.

(Source: The Economist *website*)

Exercises

Task A Review the original translation of the underlined sentences in the source text and make any necessary revisions. Then learn how to improve your revisions from the analysis and modification of the translation provided.

全球气候变暖是目前人类面临的最大挑战，围绕这一问题科学家们做出了种种预测。本文针对政府间气候变化专门委员会（IPCC）发布的气候评估报告做出评论。译文评析如下：

> 原文①②："Science has spoken," said Ban Ki-moon, the UN's Secretary-General, "time is not on our side. Leaders must act." He was reacting to the latest assessment of the state of the global climate by the Intergovernmental Panel on Climate Change (IPCC), a group of scientists who advise governments.
>
> 初译①②：联合国秘书长潘基文说："科学研究表明，时间不站在我们这边，领导人们必须要采取行动。"他回应了政府间气候变化专门委员会（IPCC）对全球气候状况的最新评估，该组织是一个为各国政府提供建议的科学家小组。

学生评改：
_____
_____
_____

> 评析：原文第一段由两个句子构成，内容是联合国秘书长对全球气候状况评估报告的评价。初译虽然传递了原文的主要信息，但连贯性较差，不符合汉语的表达习惯。首先，初译没有考虑到中西方思维方式的差异，与原文亦步亦趋，结果导致译文的可读性较差。英语习惯于直线型表达，倾向于开门见山，一般按照语义重点顺序先表态、判断，再给出结论；而汉语则反其道而行之，通常按照逻辑和时间顺序将次要信息放在句首，将语义重心放在句末。因此，改译需要根据两种语言表达习惯的不同，灵活调整句子重心。其次，初译②中的"该组织是一个为各国政府提供建议的科学家小组"

CHAPTER 8 Energy and Ecology

是对 IPCC 的介绍，按照初译的句子结构放在句末可以接受，但如果按照汉语的表达习惯调整语序后则无处安置。鉴于此，可以考虑采取加注的方法进行解决。此外，新闻或科学报告都属于正式文体，加上潘基文先生是联合国秘书长，因此在引述他的评论时，不宜使用"说"这样的词，而应采取"表示"或"称"这一类的表达。

改译：在回应联合国政府间气候变化专门委员会[1]（IPCC）对全球气候状况的最新评估时，联合国秘书长潘基文表示："科学研究表明，时间紧迫，各国领导者必须采取行动。"

注释1：政府间气候变化专门委员会是一个为各国政府提供建议的科学家小组。

原文③④：Rajendra Pachauri, the IPCC's chairman, agreed. "We have little time before the window of opportunity to stay within 2℃ of warming closes," he said. (Governments have promised not to let global temperatures rise by more than that amount compared with pre-industrial levels.)

初译③④：IPCC 主席 Rajendra Pachauri 对此表示赞同。他说："在气候变暖不超过 2℃ 的机会窗口关闭之前，我们几乎没有时间。"（各国政府已承诺，不会让全球气温上升势头超过工业化前的水平。）

学生评改：_____

评析：初译③的翻译质量较好，但初译④的问题较大。"气候变暖不超过 2℃"会让读者感到困惑，不清楚 2℃ 的具体所指。实际上，从下文括号中的解释内容可以看出，这里是指全球气温的"升幅"不超过 2℃。另外，the window of opportunity 是一种隐喻的表达方式，初译将其直译为"机会窗口"，不符合汉语的表达习惯，可以考虑从该短语的基本意义出发，将其意译为"稍纵即逝的机会"，或者使用"窗口期"这个更为专业的表达。

另外，与译文①的问题相似，译文④在引述IPCC主席的话时也使用了"他说"这样口语化的表达方式。其实"赞同"本身就含有"表达"的意思，因此没有必要重复，而是可以将两句话合并到一起。最后，括号内的译文存在一个明显的错误，即各国政府的承诺是"不会让全球气温比前工业化时期的水平高出2℃"，而非"不会让全球气温上升势头超过工业化前的水平"。之所以出现这个错误是因为初译者并未理解that amount指的就是前文提出的2℃。另外需要注意的是，在遇到外国人名时，建议不要贸然音译或保持不译，应当通过网络、新闻等查询是否已经存在译名，选择最权威、最广泛接受的译名，并在其后补充原名。

改译：IPCC主席拉金德拉·帕乔里（Rajendra Pachauri）对此表示赞同，"在将升温上升的幅度保持在2℃以内的窗口期关闭之前，我们已经没有多少时间了。"（各国政府曾承诺不会让全球气温比前工业化时期的水平高出2℃。）

原文⑤：Bill McKibben, an American climate campaigner, went for broke, calling the report "just short of announcing that climate change will produce a zombie apocalypse, plus random beheadings, plus Ebola".

初译⑤：比尔·麦吉本，一位美国气候问题的活动家，孤注一掷，说这篇报道"仅差宣布气候变化将会带来随意的斩首、埃博拉病毒以及和僵尸一样可怕的世界毁灭。"

学生评改：

评析：原文⑤是本文中翻译难度最大的一句话，其关键问题在于如何理解比尔·麦吉本对气候状况评估报告的评论。关于这一评论可以有两种理解：一种是他认为该报告没有充分地说明气候问题的严重性；另一种是他认为该报告过分夸大了气候问题的严重性。根据常识，气候变化与僵尸横行、随意斩首、埃博拉病毒根本就是"风马牛不相及"，因而可以推测麦吉本此处采取了一种诙谐、戏谑的口吻。换句话说，他认为该报告有点言过其实。据此，译者在翻译时应当将这种反讽的语气体现出来，比如将"仅差"

替换为"就差"。而短语 went for broke 译为"孤注一掷"也是不恰当的，因为这一译法根本体现不出比尔·麦吉本的态度，可以考虑将其翻译成"直言不讳"。

改译：而美国气候运动活动家比尔·麦吉本（Bill McKibben）直言不讳地指出，该报告"就差宣布气候变化将造成僵尸横行、恐怖主义肆虐，再加上埃博拉病毒蔓延了"。

原文⑥⑦：The assessment, it should be said, is sobering. But it does not justify alarmism.

初译⑥⑦：应该说的是，这份评估结果发人深省。但这并不是危言耸听。

学生评改：_____

评析：初译⑥大体上没有问题，但初译⑦出现了严重的理解错误。根据原文⑥可以看出，这份报告显示当前气候变化的形势非常严峻，令人警醒。"但这并不是危言耸听"从逻辑上来看没有问题，但从上下文语境来看是说不通的。因为上文比尔·麦吉本已经对该报告提出批评，指出它言过其实，所以此处应该与前文的基调和态度保持一致，指出该报告就是在"危言耸听"。而且，justify 的意思就是"证明……是正当的""替……辩护"，其否定结构 does not justify alarmism 理应理解为"不能证明危言耸听是合理、正当的"。

改译：应该说，这个评估是发人深省的，但决不能因此而危言耸听。

Task B Translate the following text into Chinese.

Plants in the ocean are better at storing carbon than those on land. The seagrass is more than just a biological curiosity. Along with two other kinds of coastal ecosystems—mangrove swamps and tidal marshes—seagrass meadows are particularly good at taking carbon dioxide from the air and converting it into plant matter. That makes all three ecosystems important for efforts to control climate change. This role was highlighted in a report published on March 2nd by UNESCO, an arm of the United Nations, on "blue carbon"—the sort captured by Earth's oceanic and coastal ecosystems. In total, around 33 billion tons of carbon dioxide (about three-quarters of the world's emissions in 2019) are locked away in the planet's blue carbon sinks. One reason that blue-carbon ecosystems make such effective sinks is that submerged forests are denser than their land-based equivalents. They can also trap floating debris and organic matter, which settles on the sea floor and can double the amount of carbon stored away. They possess another advantage, too. Unlike forests on land, blue-carbon ecosystems do not burn. Climate change is intensifying wildfires around the world. As forests burn, their carbon stocks are released back into the atmosphere. And fires can impede a forest's ability to capture carbon even after they have burned out. Submerged forests may be impervious to fires, but they remain vulnerable to other sorts of disasters.

Translation Tips　科技语篇翻译的衔接与连贯

　　语篇是语言交际中使用的最重要的单位之一，它由一系列连续的词语、句子和段落构成。这些语言成分并非孤立存在，而是彼此联系、相互依存，共同构成语篇这一语言整体。语篇的两大重要特征是衔接（cohesion）和连贯（coherence），它们是连词成句、择句成篇的重要保证。由于中西方思维方式的差异和英汉两种语言表达习惯的不同，译者在语篇翻译的过程中不能仅仅着眼于个别词句的选择，而应从整体全局出发，把握文章的全局脉络，深度分析上下文之间的逻辑关联，灵活采取翻译策略，最大限度实现译文的衔接和连贯。

 1. 语篇的衔接

　　衔接是指使语篇得以存在的语言成分之间的关联关系，通过词汇和语法手段使行文流畅完整、文脉相通。常用的衔接手段包括指称（reference）、替代（substitution）、省略（omission）、连接（conjunction）和词汇衔接（lexical cohesion）五种。

（1）指称

　　指称是指用简短的指代来表达上下文已经提到或即将提到的内容。英语中的指称包括人称指称（如they、he、it等）、指示指称（如this、that、those等）和比较指称（如similar、different、better等）。

（2）替代

　　替代是指语句间用一种表达来替代另一种表达的衔接手段。英语中的替代主要有名词性替代（如one替代前面指涉对象）、动词性替代（如I do中的do替代前面动作）和小句替代（I think so中的so替代前文所述内容）三种。

（3）省略

　　英语中经常出现省略现象，因为通过省略可以避免重复，实现上下文衔接。与替代相似，省略的内容可以是句子的某个成分（如名词、动词），也可以是整个小句。

（4）连接

　　使用逻辑连接词是实现语篇衔接的重要手段，科技语篇中常用的连接方式有四种：增补关系（如in addition、besides等）、转折关系（如however、although等）、因果关系（如because、therefore等），以及时间关系（如at the same time、meanwhile等）。

（5）词汇衔接

　　词汇衔接是指通过选择和使用合适的词汇来连贯文本的方式。若词汇衔接不足，则会导致文本难以阅读和理解。词汇衔接可以通过不同的方式来实现，如重复（包括重复原词、使用同义词和近义词等）、词汇搭配（包括反义、互补等）、使用连词和过

185

渡词等。有效地利用词汇衔接可以使文本更具连贯性和可理解性，从而帮助读者确定文本不同部分之间的关系。

在科技语篇翻译过程中，译者要熟悉上述衔接手段，并灵活采取各种翻译策略来实现译文与原文效果的对等。例如：

原文：**Because** safety is so important, safety standards have been established by airworthiness authorities worldwide. The latter monitors the design, development, production, operation, maintenance, and repair of any commercial aircraft to these standards. **As** there are two major authorities in the world, the FAA and EASA, it may well be that aircraft manufacturers have to comply with both of their certification requirements, which can differ from each other. **While** being absolutely mandatory, these safety standards for design clearly lead to increased product complexity.

译文：由于安全性非常重要，世界上各适航管理机构都制订了安全标准。适航机构对民用飞机的设计、研制、生产、使用和维修进行监管，使其符合适航标准。世界上有两大适航管理机构，美国的联邦航空管理局（FAA）和欧洲的欧洲航空安全局（EASA），这两个机构的适航标准有所不同，飞机制造商可以选择遵守其中一家的适航标准。这些安全性标准是强制性的，在设计中遵守这些标准会明显增加设计的复杂性。

上例中的原文由四个句子构成，其中三个句子都使用了逻辑关系词。在翻译时，考虑到汉语的形合特征，没有必要将所有连接词的意思都翻译出来，而是可以只保留第一句中的关系词 Because，并省略后面句子中的关系词 As 和 While，从而使译文表达更趋简洁。

2. 语篇的连贯

语篇承载的信息内容（如概念、事件、关系等）并不是随意拼凑、堆积在一起的，而是按照一定的逻辑顺序有机地组合在一起的，从而使语篇呈现出连贯性。在翻译的过程中，译者需要按照汉语的逻辑思维和表达习惯组织语言，调整语句的表达顺序，重新构建和组织语篇。例如：

原文：Extracting pure water from the salt solution can be done in a number of ways. One is done by distillation, which involves heating the solution until the water evaporates, and then condensing the vapor. Extracting can also be done by partially freezing the salt solution. When this is done, the water freezes first, leaving the salts in the remaining unfrozen solution.

CHAPTER 8　Energy and Ecology

译文：从盐水中提取纯水的方法有若干种。一种是加热蒸馏法，另一种是局部冷冻法。加热蒸馏法是先将盐水加热，使水分蒸发，再使蒸汽冷凝成水。局部冷冻法是使盐水部分冷冻，这时先行冷冻的是水，盐则留在未曾冷冻的液体中。

上例中的原文介绍了两种提取纯水的方法，通过使用英语中的非限制性定语从句，直接对每种方法进行了说明。在翻译成汉语时，考虑到汉语读者的阅读习惯，译文采取了"总—分"式结构，即先总体概括介绍有哪两种方法，再分述方法的具体内容。重新组合后的译文条理更加清晰，逻辑连贯性更强，也更加符合汉语的表达习惯。

Bibliography

Nida, E. (1982). *Translating Meaning*. California: English Language Institute.

Quirk, R., & Greenbaum, S. (1974). *A University Grammar of English*. London: Longman.

崔俊媛 . 2018. 语篇分析与英语阅读教学研究 . 西安：世界图书出版公司 .

方梦之 . 2011. 英语科技文体：范式与翻译 . 北京：国防工业出版社 .

李建 . 2009. 科技英语阅读与翻译 . 北京：外语教学与研究出版社 .

刘金龙，杨唯伟 . 2013. 新编科技英语阅读教程 . 北京：高等教育出版社 .

汪丽 . 2015. 新编科技英语阅读 . 广州：华南理工大学出版社 .

王大伟，魏清光 . 2005. 汉英翻译技巧教学与研究 . 北京：中国对外翻译出版公司 .

朱俊松 . 2002. 论科技英语的句法特点及翻译 . 华东船舶工业学院学报（社会科学版），（4），76–78.